THEODOR STORM SYMBOLISM

Permission granted by wildlife painter Shane Dimmick
for use of wolf image on cover is duly acknowledged.

Tellwell Talent
www.tellwell.ca

ISBN
978-1-77302-808-8 (Paperback)
978-1-77302-807-1 (eBook)

THEODOR STORM

Symbolism

READING STORM'S
LANDSCAPES

DAVID ARTISS

Acknowledgements

My debt to Storm scholarship over the past 50 years must be very evident. My Storm lectures and conversations have peripatetically crossed England, Germany, the U.S.A., Canada and South Africa and I owe much to colleagues and friends, in particular, Professors Wisbey, Brian Rowley, J.M. Ritchie and the late Professor Clifford Bernd. I wish to thank Dr. Elke Dettmer and Dr. Graham Shorrocks, part of the original *Grieshuus* research group, for their contributions. I owe a great debt to the Memorial University of Newfoundland in St. John's for its unprecedented support over the years, not least in supporting my publications. To my friend Mr. Denis C. Jackson, whose gifted and major contribution to Storm studies has sadly gone unrecognized and unappreciated in Husum,

5

unmatched, brilliant Storm translator, poet, scholar and Storm devotee that he is, I owe a profound debt for restarting my Storm batteries and cogently arguing the case for this updated reincarnation. To my wife Grace, whose D. Phil on Theodor Storm was interrupted by a serious accident, I wish to express my gratitude for all her constant support. I wish to thank Tellwell of Victoria, British Columbia for all their professional oversight in the publication of this book.

St. John's, Newfoundland & Labrador, Canada.
September, 2017

Table of Contents

Acknowledgements 5

Introduction 9

   I. Reading Storm's Landscapes 23

  II. Village Mores: The Social Landscape 45

 III. Temporal Considerations 71

 IV. The Landscape of Birds 95

  V. Of Wolves and Death: Grieshuus 125

Conclusions 143

List of Names mentioned in Text 145

Introduction

First impression of Theodor Storm's native North Friesian
landscape is one of the woods and rivers, ponds and lakes,
punts and pike-fishing anglers, wind-swept moors, derelict
water mills and small medieval towns. I was drafted to
work there in Schleswig-Holstein just after World War
Two and the experience was providential for my later
academic work on Storm. For Theodor Storm was an
iconic figure in 19th century German literature, highly
successful yet virtually unknown in England until this
recent series of brilliant, scholarly translations. There are
visual parallels to Storm's landscapes among the contemporary English painters, notably, Constable, Turner and
the Pre-Raphaelites, one of whose manifesto calls was "to
study nature attentively". Storm's nature scenery carries

undertones of Romanticism (Storm was a great admirer of Hoffmann), of Impressionism (with its emphasis on mood painting) and Realism recorded by Storm with a painter's eye, so much a part of Poetic Realism, the movement with which he is identified. This is the well-known landscape we encounter through most of Storm's novellas. It is an ambivalent, fecund and layered amalgam of critical importance when interpreting his oeuvre. As a successful lyrical poet Storm was highly conscious of the severe strictures of both time and space and these skills carried over to his narrative fiction, which is characterized by a type of impressionistic shorthand, sacrificing none of the realism yet imbuing the text with all manner of associations and allusions drawn in particular from symbolism, mythology, nature and folklore, all intricately woven into development of character, plot and sub plot. This suggests various levels of interpretation in his work, a mixture of both ambivalence and irony, yet the reader unaware of them will still be gripped, enchanted, horrified and saddened because Storm is above all, the supreme master storyteller.

By reading Storm's landscapes we sought to bring to light much that has not only been overlooked and at times denigrated in Storm scholarship but to bring into full focus powerful elements, which are frequently central to Storm's dramatic writing, particularly in the later chronicle novellas. Until very recently the extraordinary depth of Storm's animal kingdom, its all-pervading role in his major novellas together with its reflection of Storm's ethos has largely been dismissed. Two years ago an epoch-making article appeared to rectify this situation. Philipp Theisohn's 'Über Leichen gehen' 'Walking over dead bodies' discussed the role of death in Storm's work with special reference to *Zur Chronik von Grieshuus*, analyzing the latter skilfully in the exclusive terms of an 'Animal Story'. We have shown how the wolf motif dominates the tale, illuminating the central theme of the predator from first to last, symbolically embroidered by predatory birds, dogs, horses, wildlife, humans and weather. Ingrid Schuster had made similar claims in 2003, building on my own 1978 argument 'Studies in Ambivalence'. We have seen how Storm's landscapes as seen through the painter's eye are viewed consistently bifocally, in that sense the hybrid perceptions of the poet-realist. This fact alone, distinguishes Storm from all other Poetic Realists, moving him closer to Thomas Hardy, the Naturalists and the Symbolists. We have seen how Storm's range within his animal and avian kingdom is prodigious as is his manipulation of aspects facing the problem of time. The result is such that it would not only seem timely and appropriate in this Bicentenary Year of Storm's birth to recognize the timeless quality of Storm's work and deservedly elevate him to the pantheon of European literature as Master Poet and Dramatic Novelist.

Storm was fascinated by the way people furnished their homes (hence his vivid portrayal of Friesian house-interiors), with how they dressed, spun, wove and crocheted. We find descriptions of bee-keeping, coopering, hunting, distilling, farming, gardening, botanising, sculpting, painting, dyke-building, carpentering, puppeteering, and so on. He had a particularly soft spot for the way they conducted their festivities. This takes us by definition away from dilettante 'folklore' and into areas now covered by the cultural geographer and the regional ethnologist.

In one sense, of course, Storm was a product of his time. He was concerned with conservation; preservation and publication connected with dying customs, tales and songs, hence his handing over of his collection to Müllenhoff. But he was also concerned with the phylogenetic view, i.e., about every aspect of the organic growth of his Province – from its roots to its leaves, and he was not simply content with a 'historical', conserving approach.

Storm's reputation as a folklorist was already established in his lifetime - not in any international sense, as Müllenhoff's was, but certainly more than in a local one. Many aspects of the range of his folklore interests were explored by Karl Gratopp, who was able to demonstrate how far-reaching Storm's interests were. With his enthusiasm for all aspects of local folklore and super-stition fired in his early boyhood by the tales of legends recounted to him by Tante Brick and Lena Wies, Storm started collecting folksongs and folk-tales, rhymes, riddles and legends at an early age and maintained the interest for the rest of his life. He appears to have been an unusually consistent and systematic collector.

He had certain special advantages in this field: he started collecting at a very early age; his academic and legal training confirmed and strengthened a systematic approach; he had marked antiquarian instincts and a strong sense of the past; he spoke Plattdeutsch fluently and his family's reputation (largely established through the good-will of his father) together with his professional standing gave him entrée to most houses in a large area surrounding Husum, and last but not least, he clearly had the kind of personality which enabled him to mix freely with simple, working people and to make good contact with those (sometimes bizarre) characters who are frequently the vehicles for the survival of oral tradi-tion. One should also not overlook the direct influence of Storm's parental home.

His works are a monument to his erudition in the whole field of folklore and regional ethnology. All the evidence points to the fact that Storm was more than the dilettante folklorist who appears in so much of the biographical writing about him. Storm's skills place him close to the front rank of pioneer scholarly folklorists in Germany, and in many respects he should be ranked with Müllenhoff, Ludwig Bechstein and the Brothers Grimm. The distinctive feature about Storm's approach to folklore, as compared with that of his contemporaries, is the depth and breadth of his feeling for the subject. Like the twentieth century ethnographer, he demonstrated a capacity to view the subject as an integral part of the way Friesians lived.

Storm was so deeply immersed in mythology, folklore and superstition that together they became a characteristic literary mode for him. Life is frequently depicted immediately through the eyes of those who believe deeply in dark forces which control their destiny and over which they have little control. These forces may threaten their existence through some major natural catastrophe (the sea threatening their dykes is an obvious instance) or they may erupt violently within the personality of an individual, determining the direction of his other life and pointing more frequently to their (often tragic) death. Yet he is clearly able to eschew this mode when need dictates it. It is markedly absent from the 'polemical' novellas like *Im Schloß,* and from the 'aesthetic' novellas like *Psyche.*

It is notably missing from the *Unterhaltungsliteratur*[1] like *Marthe und ihre Uhr*. Yet it is very much in evidence in the *chronicle* novellas – in fact, in most of the true novellas from *Immense* through to *Der Schimmelreiter*.

Folklore and mythology permeate Storm's landscapes in both a narrow and wider sense, ranging in significance from a minor modulating role to that of thematic structure itself. It is difficult to conceive of a landscape in Storm, which is not 'orchestrated' and controlled by the underlying themes, which have their roots in folklore, superstition and mythology. It is easy to overlook the fact that this *is* an all-pervading cast of mind for Storm.

The following is not simply an attempt to identify specific elements of science, mythology, folklore and superstition in Storm's works. Nor is it in any way intended as an attempt to 'demonize' Storm – the evidence speaks for itself. But it does try to define just how characteristic those elements are in Storm's fiction – and answer not merely the question: What was this rich fund of symbols and myths that he used? – but also: Why? And How? Few Storm interpreters have addressed themselves seriously to these latter questions. The first half of this study deals with the wider implications of Storm's use of symbol, myth and superstition in a series of symbolic landscapes. In the latter

---

[1] light fiction

half, specific literary techniques in the clearly defined areas of time, birds and death come under close scrutiny.

Storm was the first to acknowledge that his prose work arose out of his poetry, particularly his love for which he was already well known by the Eighteen Fifties. Various reasons informed his choice of the novella, as his particular genre, which he described as "the sister of the drama", unrestricted by the dictates of the novel, flourishing inordinately at that time in England. He had grown up speaking fluent Danish as Schleswig-Holstein was under Danish rule for most of his childhood and had come under the influence of the Danish novellas at an early age. Yet, as he said in old age, given a second lifetime he would choose the drama as his medium. Both the advantages and challenges of the novella outweighed its restrictions: it paid well, it took less time to write than other forms, it could be produced serially in magazines and suited his hectic family life and very demanding role as a judge and it was the chosen genre of a wide circle of soon-to-be famous contemporaries such as Heyse, Keller, Stifter, Meyer, Raabe, Gotthelf, Droste-Hûlshoff and Fontane. What is harder to explain is the astonishing range of responses to Storm's fiction. He was, after all, Mao-Tse-Tung's favourite foreign author. His fellow 'Landsmann' (compatriot) Thomas Mann revered Storm, commenting on him with: "He is a master, his work will survive".

Mann's 'Buddenbrooks', the account of the steady decline in the fortunes of a Hanseatic family bears striking affinity with '*Grieshuus*'. Storm's distinction was, paradoxically, to offer hope, for he was an avowed atheist, in an age of stultifying cynicism, moribund politics and mortifying Schopenhauer pessimism. Added to this was his predilection for all forms of tragic outcome in his narratives. Yet there was no evidence in his make-up of depression, in spite of the loss in childbirth of his first wife, his muse and his cousin Constanze. With a quiver full of children he quickly married the Senator's daughter, Dorothea Jensen, with whom he had had an affair at the beginning of his marriage to Constanze, years before. For the most part he outwardly shunned all politics while corresponding with left wing friends and lending vigorous support to the 1848 revolutionaries. With the Danish reoccupation of his hometown, Husum, he was forced to leave and travel en famille to Potsdam to find work first in the Prussian Civil Service, which he hated, then to Heiligenstadt for a few years as a stipendiary magistrate. By nature a Democrat and a writer of great integrity, a profound humanitarian averse to social injustice (*A Doppelgänger*, 1886) and a noblesse oblige society, to poverty and its offspring of alcoholism and prostitution, for one of his sons was an alcoholic and the other contracted syphilis, Storm's love of his fellow man goes without saying.

Storm's interests reflect the contemporary preoccupations of a Victorian age challenged by Darwin and the new developments in science, including the urge to collect, mount and quantify as with insects and butterflies; the need to hunt big and small game, particularly birds, stuffing them and mounting them in glass cases, or caging live ones, alternatively, making a collection of thousands of bird skins. As a literary ornithologist Storm places himself in the top three of all European writers and well ahead of Shakespeare. Birds function emblematically in Storm in a variety of ways: first and foremost, he is unwavering in the integrity of his descriptions as far as science, behaviour and appearance goes, yet he will subtly use their sensory attributes such as their shape, colour(s), size, behaviour and cries as a mirror to his characters, scenes or plot development, cleverly exploiting their traditional and often dark and demonic roles in folklore and superstition. Storm shares this keen interest in folklore with Thomas Hardy together with a similar use of landscape as in 'The Woodlanders'. This combination of science and myth is paradoxical and hence, ironical. *Grieshuus* is full of paradox and irony, both situational and structural with many instances of tragic irony. Storm's debt to Heinrich Heine, whom he revered, is very apparent. A central irony in *Grieshuus* is contained in the two book structure of this novella. Storm defended this arrangement on aesthetic grounds, arguing that all the subplots and digressions pointed back to the central plot with unifying force. As a link between the two books the female figure of Matten, parallels Hinrich's life, from youth to old age, when she returns as a blind old woman with paranormal insights at the end of the tale, with links with the demented horse Fallada. Storm was to repeat this arrangement with the figure of Trin Jans in 'The Dykemaster'. The colourful range of Storm's female characters, from Elisabeth in 'Bee's Lake'to Matten and Trin Jans is a separate topic.

The last 50 years have seen such an expansion of interest in all aspects of the life and works of Theodor Storm that it can only be seen as a resounding literary phenomenon. By 1970 over 7 ½ million volumes of his works had appeared since 1945 and this figure has almost certainly doubled since then. With the Bicentenary of his birth coming up in 2017, Storm has justifiably found a place in the hearts of a wide range of readers, listeners and viewers, from the rocker young at heart to the geriatric book-lover, in the ebook, the talking book, the video, in film and stage play, article and conference, in High School, Book Club, Writer's Groups and perhaps above all on Website and Internet. There are a number of good reasons for this. First of all, there has been a steady flow of dissertations and monographs, of both paperback and hard cover biographies, of popular and academic articles, some well-edited editions of individual works and letters, several volumes of comparative criticism, numerous colourful works presenting all aspects of the Friesland topography and cultural scene. There are some items, however, which have had far-reaching influence on the man, his life and his work. First and foremost comes the Laage-Lohmeier four-volume Edition of Storm's Collected works. It is a work of outstanding team scholarship, lending a sensitive ear both to criticism of the individual work and the individual poem. Secondly, David Jackson's pioneering biography "Theodor Storm: the Life of a Democratic Humanitarian" has done much to explain that attractive side of Storm which has found an echo in the hearts of both young and old. And thirdly, filling an obvious gap in Storm studies, namely, the treatment of Storm's female characters, female scholars like Irmgard Roebling and Regina Fasold have approached the topic from several different angles and a major Swedish contribution by Louise Forssell: "Es ist nicht gut, so ganz allein zu sein…"(Stockholm, 2006) has brought us nearly up to date with her study of perceptions of masculinity and femininity in Storm's novellas.

In the 35 years since Rachel Carnaby's "Recent Trends in Theodor Storm Research" the Storm phenomenon has gone from strength to strength with a range of new post modern topics as widely diverse as the treatment of females, masculinity, questions of gender, Storm's buildings and gardens, entomological considerations and a steady flow of books and articles still preoccupied with 'Der Schimmelreiter'. David Jackson's pioneering biography had reminded me of that other outstanding biography by Robert Pitrou, read so many years ago. The only shortcoming of Jackson's book, if any, is that it leaves very little space for literary criticism, since it concentrates on the political and social science aspect of Storm's life. There is space now for a new and comprehensive volume of literary criticism encompassing Storm's verse and prose. The list of challenging paperback biographies tends to cover Storm's broader literary achievements in both genres. Among those, which stand out, are those of Bollenbeck, Fasold and Freund. Clifford Bernd's uncovering of the powerful influence on Storm of the Danish novella broke new ground; together with his far-reaching discussion of European Poetic Realism. Concurrent with all of this have been the many physical improvements to the Stormhaus and Archive and its furniture and garden. Finally, mention must be made of the series of approximately seventeen Storm novellas, brilliantly translated into English by the award-winning Storm specialist and translator, Dennis C. Jackson, due to appear in paperback and e-book in 2017, including his final translation of *Zur Chronik von Grieshuus*.

CHAPTER I

Reading Storm's Landscapes

Much of the diversity and regionalism of the Schleswig-Holstein scene is to be found reflected in Storm's landscapes when one thinks of shore and dyke, his dotting of local islands in the sea, expansive moor, extensive forest and woods, scenes of war and devastation and defended bridges and water ways. And yet the colourful vast vista is rarely to be found in any great detail for he is really more interested in human habitations, from the dilapidated hovel at one extreme, through the well established family homes of Husum to the luxury of Manor House and castle at the other, all of which suffer from the devastating attacks of time. So what we are considering here are essentially the landscapes of nature and the natural scene, of the social scene, of how he treats the landscape of time and of the larger landscape of history. It is argued that the literary technique, which he develops with regard to his treatment of nature, distinguishes him from all other Poetic Realists. At the root of it is the rare combination in Storm of the expert naturalist – the ornithologist, mammologist, ichthyologist, entomologist, dendrologist and botanist and at the other end the truly expert folklorist and mythologist with an extensive knowledge of all aspects of superstition and deviltry. For the combination of these skills completely undermines the landscape innocence perceived by most of Storm's readers. There is overwhelming evidence that Storm used a system of signs and symbols, which enables us to chart his landscape virtually in cartographic terms. It could be argued that he is that type of chart maker who embroiders his sea with denizens of the depths, his terrain with the appropriate flora and fauna and his skies with birds on the wing. Yet even this image would be very misleading, for it smacks of the popular and purely decorative, the shallow and the scientifically inaccurate, which is to do Storm great injustice.

In his penetrating study on how powerful Darwinian thinking influenced Storm through close examination of death in all its forms in Storm's work by clinically examining all references to death (violent and otherwise), suicide, accident, murder, war, and starvation, Philipp Theisohn recognises like an itinerant coroner what central significance predatory and non-predatory animals and birds play in Storm's oeuvre. He suggests that Storm is following Darwin in propounding that man in the evolutionary process is an animal and that his behaviour confirms much of the notion 'the survival of the fittest'. He claims justifiably that the teleological implications of *Grieshuus* are embedded in the fact that the story is concerned with animals and death for all the superstitions surrounding dogs, wolves, horses and predatory birds point in one direction only and that is to death. The philosophical implications for Storm are complex and there are several caveats to this argument, which I will try to address in my chapter 5 on *Grieshuus*. But the final recognition by a noted Storm scholar of the fundamental and frequently sinister role of animal and bird in Storm's work would seem to give support to my bifocal view. Theisohn also points out that while Storm appears to follow Darwin in accepting man's predatory nature, a significant traditional line can be found in Poetic Realism which begins to rediscover man as animal. A response to his discussion of *Grieshuus* will follow in my chapter 5.

The literary exploitation and symbolic manipulation of landscape is undeniably one of the major features of

Storm's craft as a writer. His landscapes have been the subject of a plethora of critical attention. The question arises: is Storm's scenery really so innocuous? In the light of his known interest in mythology and his expert knowledge of – and commitment to – folklore, much that is superficially light, even gay and innocent on the surface takes on a darker, more sinister aspect, when evaluated from the folklorist's point of view. He is that type of chart-maker who embroiders his seas with denizens of the depths, his terrain with the appropriate flora and fauna and his skies with birds on the wing. Yet even this image would be very misleading for it smacks of the popular and purely decorative, the shallow and the scientifically inaccurate, which is to do Storm great injustice. Storm's charts are painstakingly wrought and highly consistent in scientific terms. That is to say that Storm the naturalist is committed to the accurate, consistent and scientific representation of nature. He is not normally prepared to take liberties with the laws of nature. Exceptions to this occur in the *Märchen* or in the distortion of nature in the folk-take – a distortion that is seen as an aberration of the popular mind. By means of this latter device, Storm is able to stand personally aloof. At the same time, Storm's charts are uniquely emblematic and reflect a novel brand of poetic realism.

When Thomas Kuchenbuch wrote of a "dialectic of illusion and disillusion" in Storm's work, he had his finger on the pulse of most of Storm's landscape images. Only rarely – and that in the better criticisms of Storm, do we find this awareness of the tensions in his landscapes and of the fact that Storm is rarely, if ever, concerned simply with a detailed, realistic representation of nature, but that landscape is inextricably bound up in his novellas with overall design, plot and character. Landscape as a major atmospheric medium, as a companion to and intensifier of events, as a mirror to the 'souls' of his characters, and as a vehicle and stimulus for human feelings and thoughts – these aspects have been recognized. But it seems to me that a major aspect of Storm's landscape technique has been overlooked. What Storm has done in his landscapes, under the smokescreen of authentic, convincing and realistic backcloths, is to marry a symbol-system with a refined, literary technique, namely, the demonization of nature.

In this preoccupation with the demonic Storm's debt to the Romantics in general and Eichendorff in particular becomes very apparent, but his synthesis of Romantic theme and technique with methods so realistic as to border on the naturalistic makes his contribution to this art form unique. When Reitz suggested that it is only in isolated instances that Storm depicts elements of the weird, the phantastic, the sinister and the demonic, he was only expressing a major misconception.

Symbolic aspects of the sinister and demonic feature in virtually all of Storm's landscapes, certainly in all of the 'true' novellas in varying degree. What must be taken into account is a fundamentally ironic view of nature, present in Storm's work from *Immensee* on.

Storm's natural landscapes, therefore, require a special focus of attention. An understanding of his attitude to nature is critically important when attempting to come to terms with his symbolic landscapes. The essence of Storm's relationship to nature lies in his bifocal view. It is essentially a tragic-idyllic, bittersweet affair – not in any conventional sense – and justice has not been done to its bitterness. Clifford Bernd has noted the heavy preponderance of the themes of pain and melancholy running right through Storm's narrative work, analyzing Storm's special kind of melancholy and tracing it back to the Romantics. But it is generally argued that bitterness only creeps in after the death of his wife, Constanze, when Storm moves into the second major phase of his writing and begins to lean towards what is frequently called the tragic. This fate novella view can only be described as at best misleading. We shall see that Storm's view of nature was full of irony in a Heineesque way from *Immensee* onwards. Virtually all of his nature descriptions are imbued with a deep sense of bitterness, and nature harboured very few 'sentimental' illusions for Storm at all.

It is particularly in Storm's response to nature that the range of his imagery can best be observed for his nature images outnumber all others by two to one. As we watch the patterns of symbols, images and motifs, drawn exclusively from nature, emerging, it becomes clear that we are faced with a writer who is not merely a sensitive observer and faithful recorder – which Storm undoubtedly was – but with someone who is using nature in an exceedingly sophisticated way both as a foil to his own thought and as a foil to his characters. A close analysis of Storm's nature symbols explodes the myth of a colourful, regional, quaint and innocuous backcloth to much of his writing. It is just because Storm's symbols are so unobtrusive and 'natural' that they blend so masterfully into the landscape of his writing. They are a far call from those obtrusive "pseudosymbols" which depend on explicatory pointers; rather are they essential component parts woven into the fabric of the story and part of it matrix. Storm's birds are a case in point. They are occasionally incidentals in a story; more frequently part of a bird motif and on half a dozen occasions, symbols central to the plot of the novella. But at no point does the reader sense that they have been 'inserted' to embellish the story.

There is no doubt that Storm was particularly sensitive in his response to all aspects of nature. This sensitivity cannot be explained away simply by pointing to the nineteenth-century preoccupation with the Natural Sciences – with collecting and classifying, stuffing and mounting, something of which is admittedly reflected in Storm's works. It is rather to be seen in Storm's own temperament and proclivities. He spent the summers of his youth at his grandfather's mill in the country; he was fully acquainted with sea and seashore life through living in Husum; he was deeply attached through local patriotism to Schleswig-Holstein. He was an acute observer from his youth, with an eye for colour and line. He was possessed of acute hearing and was very gifted musically (later directing his own choir in Husum and Heiligenstadt). He was a very good amateur ornithologist and an excellent botanist. Markedly sensual by nature, he was essentially a Gefühlsmensch (person of feeling). In saying all this one is saying nothing new, but it needs restating at this juncture because the consideration of Storm's relationship to nature is crucial when attempting to come to terms with his symbolic landscapes.

Alexander Pache drew attention to hidden depths in Heine's landscapes and pointed out striking similarities between Heine and Storm not long after the turn of the century. He noted particularly their common ability to draw on motifs from Germanic mythology and re-create them in a new form. His comments on Heine's hypersensitivity, narrow horizon and extraordinary powers of concentration remind one of similar phenomena in Storm. Storm, however, with his view of existence as a continuum, does present a more overall view of life, pointing to past, present and future. Pache writes also at this point of Heine's 'nervous way of perceiving visually'. It is a telling phrase, equally applicable to Storm. Heine, a fellow devotee of roses, shares Storm's capacity for a special kind of binocular vision: the simultaneous awareness of beauty and loathing. One is forced to certain conclusions concerning Storm's Heineesque view of nature. The themes of alienation, solitude and death clearly lie at the heart of Storm's work. Moreover one of Storm's major techniques is to be found in his demonization of nature. Furthermore, Storm's awareness of the transience of life is so acute that it extends not only to the majority of his characters but particularly to nature as well. It is not difficult to demonstrate the fundamental significance of alienation, solitude and death in Storm's work. Aspects of all three themes have been treated in past Storm scholarship. Yet only certain criticism singles out alienation or solitude – and even the solipsistic doubt – as the hallmark of Storm's narrative writing. The view that love and death are the two main themes in Storm's work can be found, with variations, in most Storm criticism, from the earliest to the most recent. It is true; Storm achieves much of the tension in his work through the polarization of love and death. He reflects this antinomy in nature very skilfully. It is brilliantly reflected, for example, in his bird imagery, where a full range of death images appears in the guise of certain species, like the owl, the crow and the magpie, while traditional symbols of love, like the nightingale, the linnet, and the lark are employed both conventionally and ironically, to underscore the bitter-sweet tragedy of existence. It is particularly at moments of delight that we are likely to meet immediate, deft qualifications, as, for example, when Hauke Haien's new dyke is making excellent progress and the larks are singing high in the sky: "Hauke, who was unaware of how nature can deceive us with its charms, stood at the Northwest corner." Nature, until inspired by the poet, is essentially a sepulchral arena for Storm. He is not interested in depicting nature per se; what he wishes to convey is the effect nature has on him. He knows that nature is just as much a merciless battleground as is the sphere of human relations in society at large. It is in his irony that this is best expressed. The death of a main character is frequently foreshadowed by the description of a ball or some similar festivity and so the Dance-of-Life becomes a Dance-of-Death.

But when all is said and done love and death are hardly original themes in any writer's vocabulary. The distinctive feature of Storm's work seems to me not that he frequently handles the twin themes of love and death very skilfully but that behind it all lie metaphysical problems with which he wrestled from youth to the grave, namely, the problems of alienation, solitude and mortality.

Thomas Kuchenbuch appears to me to be getting close to the mainsprings of Storm's landscapes when he suggests at the beginning of his study that the tensions in them are really the tensions of the epoch, between a subjective viewpoint and an intended objective one. His argument owes much to Fritz Martini. Storm never managed to reconcile these two aspects of life. His attempts to bridge the abyss between the subjective world of sense impressions and the so-called objective facts of existence, between the ideal and the real always appear to end in failure. The striking fact is that he continued to make the attempts to the end. By the end of his life, he was more reconciled to a "continuity in change" approach to life, which conceded the place of ugliness, decay, corruption and death as counter poles of beauty, growth, health (life) and love.

T.J. Rogers, in a brilliant discussion of Storm's literary connections, attempts to lay the ghost, which haunts most literary criticism of the period – that spectre which arises from all discussion of the 'subjective' and 'objective' elements of Poetic Realism. Tracing the phenomenon outlined by Brinkmann in *Reality and Illusion,* he shows how the Goethean assurance of the ideal within the real – the discovery of the universal in the particular – is lost and a process of disintegration sets in, whereby it is recognized just how subjective the reproduction of an 'objective' reality can be – and the terms 'subjective' and 'objective' become interchangeable and interdependent. Storm, he argues, is acutely aware of the disconnection identified by J.P. Stern in *Re-Interpretations,* - a disconnection that exists in the creative German mind between the individual sensibility and the world outside it, and in this sense Storm is at one with the writers discussed by Stern:

"Storm's work points again and again to that disconnection, that uncertainty about the substance of the objective world; in his quiet way he leads us more directly to the edge of the chasm between subject and object, and makes us more strongly aware that we are on the edge, than perhaps any other writer of his time. His writing is about the chasm, and his fundamental concern is to show and drive home the fact that it exists and is frightening; for the most part he does not create a world of his own away from the edge, nor claim to propose clear ways of throwing a bridge (illusory or effective) across to the other side. He does, it can be claimed, offer provisional values to set against his ultimate doubt, but I do not think we have the sense that he is ever deceived by what he offers, ever satisfied, in a way unsatisfactory to us, that any of these values really provides a final solution."

Love may be the rose and death the worm in the rose but what of life itself, if at the end of it all, man is just snuffed out like a candle? The question surfaces markedly during his courtship and correspondence with Constanze.

If one looks at the majority of Storm's central characters, one cannot help noticing they are all people nursing existential problems of this nature, from Marthe talking to her clock, Reinhard in love with the idea of being in love with Elisabeth (but incapable of action) in *Immensee*, and Harre Jensen, nursing his guilt, solitude and youthful love for the girl he left behind, Ehrhard in *Angelika*, driven to the ultimate realization he is alone, and Anne Lene, alienated from local society by her inheritance and condemned to solitude and death in *Auf dem Staatshof*, right through to Hauke Haien's alienation from the community and bitter struggle with the forces of darkness in *Der Schimmelreiter*. The vast majority of Storm's lovers, for example, are for one reason or another unsuccessful: many are unable to establish a meaningful relationship, and for those who do, the relationship must inevitably founder on some external, fate-established reef. Marthe never finds a meaningful relationship and ends up talking to her clock, Reinhard and Elisabeth circle like Greek wrestlers, never establishing a satisfactory relationship, and their lives suffer as a consequence. The young man in *Posthuma* "is forced to love a dead girl because he is unable to relate to the girl while she is alive." Fränzchen and Konstantin's attempt to come together in *Im Sonnenschein* is thwarted by an impossibly imperious father, Ehrhard can never come to terms with Angelika: when at last she is free he realizes he does not want her anyway. Renate and Josias are frustrated in their love by superstition and social hostility. So the list goes on, right through Storm's work. The number of couples who work out a meaningful relationship in harmony with society is infinitesimal: Arnold and Anna in *Im Schloß*, Rudolf and Anna in *Schweigen*, Rudolf and his unnamed wife in *Späte Rosen*. Others might have succeeded, but the wife dies in childbirth or comes to a violent end. Occasionally love goes unrequited and the resolution may be that of (contented?) resignation (*Drüben am Markt*) or fatalistic acceptance (*Waldwinkel*).

All these characters, far from being the products of a sentimental view of existence, seem to me to be the projections of a mind characterized by its scepticism and deep sense of irony. As Terence Rogers eloquently puts it apropos of Storm's tentative advance from scepticism to hope: "And that hope is the finer for having been carved out of hopelessness." Death had always preoccupied

Storm; to this theme was added that of solitude on Constanze's death, if not before.

"Solitude and the torturing riddle of death, these are the two terrible powers with which I am battling unceasingly in silence".

It was a struggle he maintained for the rest of his life.

The struggle finds characteristic expression in Storm's technique of employing nature as the most effective vehicle for the demonic element, which is present in most of his narrative work.

This technique of demonization has been noted with regard to heath descriptions and the gardens in Storm's work but the technique is central to Storm's work as a whole. It operates markedly in *Immensee*, and runs through the majority of Storm's novellas gaining all the time in sophistication and effect. That the demonic aspect, which is so central to Storm's work, should have received such scant attention is a further enigmatic feature of Storm scholarship, especially in the light of Storm's erudition and known interest in this field. It is true that just where Storm's nature descriptions are at their most plastic and seemingly innocuous, the demonic element is most likely to be met with – surely one of Storm's subtler ironies. That is not to suggest its complete neglect in Storm studies. It is just that some critics appear to be more receptive to its role than others. What I do suggest is that the demonic, especially as presented through the medium of nature, with its roots in superstition, folklore and mythology and its specific connection in Storm's mind with the "Poesie des Lebens" – the demonic element, far from being a peripheral curiosity in Storm's work, constitutes one of the most significant themes to be traced throughout both his prose and his verse. It is specifically in this technique of the demonization of nature that Storm is inimitable.

Considerable attention has been devoted to Storm's sense of the transience of life. Both Tilo Alt and Clifford Bernd consider that transience, with its related phenomenon of anxiety poses the major psychological problem for Storm's characters and reflects Storm's lifelong preoccupation with this theme. His taste for Baroque literature and the seventeenth century in general is reflected in his works by an acute sense of evanescence. His sensitivity to the 'sudden death' atmosphere of the seventeenth century makes his work all the more comprehensible to twentieth century readers. The 'rosy glow' that emanates from some of his writing must be taken as poetic irony very much in a Heine vein – a smokescreen, concealing a view of life, which is racked with pain at the thought of the ineluctable passing of all beauty – and time. Storm can scarcely view his favourite flower, the rose in full bloom, without simultaneously being painfully aware of such beauty withered, wilted and faded. Therein also lies the ambivalence of his view: Nature is dead until inspired, passive but beautiful, for Man life is solitude and pain alleviated by beauty. One thinks of that much-quoted sentence found towards the end of *Auf dem Staatshof*, in this context:

"and I was overcome with that shudder which is so wonderfully mixed between the longing for earthly pleasure and the painful feeling of its transience."

The 'speaker' is Marx and the passage immediately precedes Anne Lene's sudden death. *Auf dem Staatshof* was written in 1857 and the passage reveals an awareness of the bitter irony of transience even in the early novellas. *Immensee* particularly, is deeply imbued with a sense of transience and the loss of what might have been. Storm's view of nature is cradled in ambivalence right from the beginning. It is characterized by a deep, poetic sensitivity to all beauty and an equally penetrating scepticism with regard to the bitter foundation upon which all beauty rests. It is this antinomy which is the mainspring of most of Storm's nature symbolism, and which generates the dialectic of his symbolic landscapes.

In trying to come to terms with Storm's symbols, yet another factor must be taken into consideration. Theodor Storm was a man of demonstrably eclectic tastes. His interests ranged through natural history, Classical and Germanic mythology, superstition and the occult and the literatures of several European countries. It is not surprising that elements of this eclecticism turn up regularly in his work. What is surprising is that they have not been studied more systematically than they have, for a systematic study would have shown that running through most of Storm's narrative fiction at subsurface level is a system of folkloric symbols indicating that most of his descriptive nature passages are coded. As one proceeds to crack this code it becomes clear that one is faced with a writer who is using a highly sophisticated technique – so sophisticated that the full complexities would escape all but the most searching inquiry. The 'innocent' landscape, for instance, was found to be heavily compromised and the language of its scenery so distinctly loaded that it might be operating at several independent levels. Nowhere was it found to be operating more concentrated than in the two areas of natural science and mythology.

Science and mythology play a central role in virtually all of Storm's narrative works. If one were searching for a literary hallmark for Storm, one would have to look no further. His masterly blending of science and myth is inimitable. It springs from two of the consuming interests of his life: a lifelong fascination for the natural sciences – for lepidopterology, botany and ornithology – and a seemingly congenital disposition towards all aspects of mythology and folklore. This is a curious and paradoxical combination of interests: it must be difficult to reconcile a total devotion to the systematic techniques of applied science with a fascination for ghosts, witchcraft, superstition and the occult. Newton, it is true, had secretly achieved a similar synthesis two centuries earlier. The astonishing thing about Storm is that he somehow manages to do it without compromising his reputation as a very sober and down-to-earth lawyer. He nevertheless takes out certain insurances. The most common one is in the form of a smokescreen of distance not only between himself, the author, and all superstitious utterances but also between the narrator and the expression of superstitious belief. This gives him the cover of a second-hand or third-hand account (see *Der Schimmelreiter*), the reliability of which is then thrown into doubt. Another technique is to place the expressions of belief in the supernatural or dark forces in the mouth of compromised characters – mindless servants and semi-deranged women, gypsies or broken-down recluses. Yet a further technique is to use characters that have had some brush with primitive religion – particularly with sects whose practices are characterized by religious hysteria.

The use of 'landscape' in the context of Storm's physical landscapes requires clarification. We are not thinking here so much of an extensive view of a natural scene, a vista or panorama, though these are also to be found in Storm's work (a notable example would be the brilliantly evocative description of the Heide, found by the narrator in the posthumous effects of the Old Cousin in *Eine Halligfahrt*". We are thinking more in terms of a narrowing-down of the panoramic view to a forest setting, a farmhouse garden or a vicarage pond. They become in effect a landscape within a landscape, in the sense that Wolfgang Baumgart speaks of the forest as landscape in his monograph *Der Wald in der deutschen Dichtung* (Berlin, 1936), page 4:

"It (the forest) has the unique quality depending on the view of the beholder on the one hand part of the landscape on the other occasion to be landscape itself."

The panoramic view is relatively scarce in Storm's work; one suspects that it was too much of a Romantic stereotype for Storm's sensibilities. One of the illusions Storm creates is that his novellas are permeated with excursive narrative depicting extensive, panoramic views. But this is the reverse of the truth. His landscapes mostly appear in short bursts of heavily concentrated and narrowly circumscribed mood paintings. We hear much of the dykes and dyke building in *Der Schimmelreiter* but it is we who conjure up the vistas of the *Wattenmeer*. Panoramic views do occur, of course, - Reinhard approaching *Immensee* from the hill above is just one example. Brief descriptions of sunsets on expansive horizons are others. What we are concerned with here is in examining Storm's use of landscape in carefully circumscribed terms – his manipulation of landscape as nature image.

In this Bicentenary Year of Theodor Storm's birth it is prudent to take stock of some of these quintessential elements in Storm's oeuvre, which distinguish him from all of his European contemporaries except for one. Any comparative study of the landscapes to be found in the fiction of both Theodor Storm and the English novelist Thomas Hardy reveals not only their common sense of loss at the disappearing landscape but also their mutual concept of the depiction of nature, revealing them alone among contemporary European writers as close kindred spirits. They were both expert folklorists and both excellent natural scientists. The striking parallels in their use of nature imagery to develop the structure of a specific topographical scene, mirroring techniques used by the English landscape painters, such as Constable, Ruskin and Burne-Jones, only serve to underscore the affinity of these two writers. This is not to suggest that we overlook and devalue the memorable landscapes of the other Poetic Realists such as Stifter's magnificent evocation of the Hungarian Puszta or Gotthelf's farm scenes. Storm was particularly distressed by the loss of the Heide which had featured as such a large part of his childhood and youth and Hardy was so preoccupied with the central role of Egdon Heath in 'The Return of the Native' that he could only bemoan its gradual disappearance. Two works help to clarify this connection: Ernst Hebart, "The Function of Nature and Symbolism and their Relationship to Man in the Works of Theodor Storm and Thomas Hardy" (diss. University of Adelaide, 1965) and Michael Irwin's brilliant study: 'Reading Hardy's Landscapes', (London, 2000) though not mentioning Storm, contains so many striking parallels as he examines with a fine-toothed comb such disparate topics as Insects, Noises, Poetry of Motion, Erosion, Deformation and Reformation (of landscape), alerting us to both proximity and contrast in the treatment of both Heide and Heath.

While Storm's fascination for and manipulation of birds is matched by Thomas Hardy's predilection for and extensive knowledge of insects, Hardy's limited deployment of birds helps to reinforce our reading of Storm's use of them, such is the great disparity in the way they handle them. For Hardy they represent a diversion, an excuse to expand on their migratory habits and the chance to elaborate on far-flung, exotic topographical regions as disparate as the Arctic and Africa, in other words as an opportunity for digression. Storm's birds are usually solitary, behaviourally accurate and in their duplicity, poetically highly significant.

CHAPTER II

Village Mores: The Social Landscape

The kind of symbolic view we have been discussing in the previous chapter is seen to good advantage in one of the lesser known of Storm's novellas *Draußen im Heidedorf*[1] expanded into a wider landscape, the social landscape of a tightly-knit village community. Now, however, the irrational comes very much into evidence. The demonic now takes on a central role. Yet it is in many ways subsumed and concealed by the space given to social interaction. There is something new here for Storm. First of all, there is the

---

[1] Out in the Village on the Heath

daring juxtaposition of a very pretty girl with the bestial images of vampire and werewolf – a development that Fritz Böttger believed would have been impossible prior to 1870. Then there is the extended reliance on village superstition, which was to become such a feature of the later novellas. Thirdly, there is a new materialistic exploration of an aspect of the love-relationship, which he had not treated before. Whether one calls it an irresistible sexual attraction or a self-destructive fixation is neither here nor there. The point is there does appear to be a new sense of disillusionment about the love-relationship, which gives greater credence to the irrational and illogical aspects of human behavior.

The contradictions and paradoxes, which are the essence of human behavior never ceased to fascinate Storm. Acutely conscious of the polarity of all life – a characteristic he shares with Goethe and Hesse – Storm observes, carefully records and marvels at not only man's lesser foibles but also his more destructive passions. Though a professional lawyer, he rarely sits in judgment on his fictional characters, taking up an impartial position and allowing his separate narrators to express their own judgment. *Draußen im Heidedorf* is one of Storm's more finely wrought tales, which has its origins in a case, which came before him in his capacity as district judge in Husum. It is a story in which Storm's characteristic techniques of multiple narration, demonic leitmotif, economy, nature symbolism and subtle lighting combine effectively with his legal expertise to produce a result remarkable both for its psychological insight and a certain compelling tragic grandeur. Storm strikes a new note with this "drama of country passion." Its journalistic approach, in which the district judge 'reports' on not only his cross examinations of witnesses but also on his own conversations and observations and begins to build up from the early fragmented evidence a composite picture of the tragedy – this journalistic approach gives a down-to-earth, fresh impression of realism and objectivity which had so far escaped Storm.

The opening scene is typically impressionistic, solely (and highly effectively) illuminated by hand lanterns, which swing along the dark, narrow streets like will-o'-the –wisps. It is very evocative and not a little atmospheric. One stationary lantern attracts the Judge's attention, so he pauses and observes the brief human scene, which plays before him, with a direct apology to the reader. This brief interlude enables Storm to permit the three main characters in his story to introduce themselves: the Judge-narrator who remains anonymous, a young farmer called Hinrich and a pretty girl with pointed teeth called Margret. We learn that Hinrich, with his prominent brow, has a broody look about him. There is a brief *brouillerie* between the young people, as to where the girl is going to sit in the cart – next to the older woman or next to the young farmer. The latter brusquely insists on the girl joining him at the front, and then whips up the horses violently, clattering off down the street and smashing the mounting- stool in the process.

What we have learnt about these characters has been strictly circumscribed by the darkness and the restrictions thus placed on the Judge's view – by the light of the lantern. He is, for instance, only able to see the lower half of Margret's face with her dark eyes and pale face, her teasing wilfulness about sitting next to Hinrich, her white teeth and full lips so she already has the makings of one of Storm's *femmes fatales*. In spite of the darkness, then, and with a remarkable economy of line we already have a meaningful image of the protagonists. A few brief glimpses by lantern-light have sufficed.

How different this technique is from traditional contemporary character portrayal.

Storm deftly conveys a rapid series of sense-impressions, out of which emerges a pointed contrast between his protagonists: on the one hand, the trimly built, dark-eyed beauty, on the other, the boorish, impetuous and violent young farmer. The whole scene has explicitly magic lantern quality about it – a brief shadow play which sticks in the narrator's memory.

The crux of the matter in *Draußen im Heidedorf* is the conflict between the demands made on a simple young farmer by his narrow, conservative, tightly structured, agrarian society on the one hand and the passion he conceives for an alien girl, on the other. This conflict is predestined to be a tragic one because it is born of irreconcilable opposites. These are what might be called the 'territorial imperative' to secure his family's land-tenure (and future) by marrying a girl ten years his senior, for whom he has no regard but who has land and money – and the 'demonic imperative' which compels him to take his own life when he realizes that he can never marry the girl for whom he has conceived an all-consuming passion. The fact that it is questionable whether the girl reciprocates his feelings is presented as irrelevant.

The conflict is an interesting one in the context of Storm's work up to this point, for it has not only human, psychological interest but also sociological and philosophical implications as well. Up to and including *Eine Halligfahrt* local and village society depicted in Storm's work can generally be seen to be a very stable structure, with longstanding traditions, a recognizable hierarchy and a rigid system of inheritance. In *Draußen im Heidedorf* this society is shown for the first time to be vulnerable to irrational forces beyond its control. The sexton and his wife, who represent inviolable bourgeois continuity, are responsible for suggesting the solution, which ultimately takes Hinrich to his death. The solution preserves the order but the latter has already shown it to be vulnerable. In this sense there is a 'new look' about Storm's work. It is fair to assume that the successive personal crises of exile, loss of Constanze and the urgent need to replace her contributed to a tempering of the earlier optimism. Storm gradually becomes increasingly reconciled to the idea that the old established 'Victorian' order is crumbling, without necessarily relinquishing all hope. The harmony had been shattered but the result was a tougher, crystallized form of realism. Martini sees this as verging on the pathological; Stuckert regards it as a natural development in his writing. Gertrud Storm claims her father was aware of a new depth and breadth in his writing. The real point is surely not how the development occurred but the fact that he could now treat the effects of a tragic passion dispassionately. Setting out to prove that he could write without elegiac *Stimmung*, he has made his point overwhelmingly.

One of the key results of this development in style is the new sense of urgency in the text, necessitating an even more severe form of economy. Sentences are shortened, conjunctions and dependent clauses used sparingly. A sense of pace is generated which develops a momentum carried right through the story. Though it is a 'legal' story, quite the opposite effect of the slow, grinding wheels of justice is obtained. Here we have a local District Judge carrying out his duties efficiently and smoothly with a minimum of fuss. Once the introductions have been made, the plot thickens instantly, as it were.

The plot centres around the young farmer Hinrich Fehse, whose father has just died leaving his farm deeply in debt. The District Judge calls a meeting to discuss the affairs of the family, at which the Sexton announces that arrangements have already been made for the young farmer to marry a propertied girl in the village, so that they can then farm both properties and pay off the debts. The Judge cannot understand why the young man is so depressed about the arrangement until he recalls that Fehse was the man he had seen six months previously driving off on the cart. The observation is significant in that the judge, in passing a value judgment on Margret, compromises his own neutrality and thereby becomes one of the 'personalities' in the story (not in any sense an omniscient narrator) and the central conflict is neatly epitomized by the juxtaposition of the "dangerous" girl with the "sullen young man". The theme is developed and pursued inexorably. We learn first from the judge that the girl is a midwife's daughter from a neighboring village and is "especially pretty". The sexton informs us that she is to be sent away to work in the nearby town, that she would in any case be incapable of "solider Bauernarbeit",[1] that the arrangement has been brought about by a special payment, that the girl has in any case no dowry and a pretty face is not much use in the situation, that her grandfather was a Slovak from the Danube, her midwife mother a card-player and fortune-teller, in short, it would be highly unsuitable match for an old farming family. Furthermore, there was the question of whether the girl would have accepted him as she already had others 'in tow'. Whether this is all true or not, we don't know. We have a suspicion that the sexton is not exactly in favour of Margret.

The point of this seemingly mechanical recapitulation of the plot is that in the space of a brief paragraph Storm has forcefully developed his theme of the "dangerous girl", as she is reflected through a pattern of allusions in the eyes of a local, previously described as "nur allzu weltklug"[2]. The reflections may be slightly out of focus but it is the way the locals regard her. The picture is pretty damning. Margret is beautiful and lazy, a dangerous 'gypsy' of dubious descent; she would be incapable of working a farm and could bring no dowry to it. She is 'flighty', would not necessarily accept Hinrich and has several strings to her bow. The whole picture is a reflection of

[1] "rugged farmers' work"

[2] "only too worldlywise"

local prejudice and parochialism, based on the juxtaposing between "upright, honest God-fearing Friesians" and "lazy, loose, heathen gypsies." The dangerous fascination which Margret already exerts on Hinrich is seen at the conclusion of this scene, where we find Hinrich in a catatonic state, finally putting his signature to the document "wie von der eisernen Notwendigkeit am Draht gezogen"[1] crystallizes the clash of the two imperatives in a single sentence introduced with "Vor seinem inneren Auge". The device is typical of Storm, not simply because the phrase "vor seinem inneren Auge"[2] is a favourite one. It is just because this oblique method of stating this novella's *Problematik* is so oblique – by placing it speculatively as a tentative thought in the mind of the main character – that it is so effective. The two images of voluptuous girl and farming taboo touch the heart of the matter.

The sexton's wife virtually steals this scene because she is the link between the legend and the main characters. She is depicted as a villager subscribing to local legend and superstition and as such she is one of a long line of characters in Storm's work. She has perhaps most in common with Trin Jans in *Der Schimmelreiter*, the key, demonic link figure in the novella, for Storm takes pains to stress

[1] "as if pulled by wire by iron necessity"

[2] "before his inner eye"

certain ominous characteristics about her – the little, bent, old, sickly figure with the bony hands, sitting behind the lighted stove, almost covered by her woolen shawl. She is racked with lumbago and shouts to the maid in a "sharp" voice. The real clue as to Storm's intentions, however, may be found in the single reference to the tripod with all its known cult associations and its specific use against witchcraft. It is also an image of genuine plastic realism.

Hinrich Fehse, whose fortunes never looked very bright, is now hell-bent on a downward path that must inevitably lead to tragedy. The incident with the Jutland horse-trader, overlooked and accounted for by the judge, in which Hinrich trades in two fine brown cart-horses for a pair of rundown hacks, neatly mirrors his physical and mental condition, for their forlorn, hangdog expression is an animistic echo of their new owner, whose face has become "scharf und mager,"[1] whose eyes have practically disappeared beneath the protruding brow and who now looks in local parlance as if he has "böse verspielt".[2] After Hinrich is found squandering his new found wealth on gifts and clothes for Margret, who has returned to the village after six months, arrangements are made for the property to be placed under trusteeship.

[1] "sharp and gaunt"

[2] "got into bad ways"

At this point Hinrich is declared missing and the judge decides to investigate.

A section follows of three paragraphs in which Storm exploits the natural setting characteristically for premonitory purposes. The technique is simple but nonetheless effective. It is autumn as the judge sets out with a clerk in a pony and trap. The scene appears harmless enough at first, though there are life-and-death undertones in the reference to the decisive coming of winter.

The passing reference to a spindle-tree also appears harmless enough until we probe a little further. Our suspicions are slightly aroused when the judge describes the scene as "schwermütig"[1] as he watches the yellow leaves falling in the sunshine. When a late thrush, startled by the snorting of the horses, utters its 'cry of fear', we note that the thrush is traditionally a familiar of the devil. Angstschrei[2] has its own subconscious effect. Reference to the "Wilden Moor" is not exactly calculated to cheer us up. Piles of turves tower up out of the desolate scene beside solitary ponds. From time to time they hear the melancholy cry of the *Große Regenpfeifer*. Storm almost certainly intended this to refer to the curlew[3] and its

---

[1] despondent

[2] cry of fear

[3] where the Plattdeutsch clearly indicates this bird

traditional European role as a death warning. With its wider associations with the Wild Huntsman and the Seven Whistlers, it is a singularly felicitous choice both as the sensuous culminating image of this coded, premonitory passage of nature description and as the final introduction to the sinister element, which immediately follows.

The scene reminds the narrator of a story he had heard which came from the Slav-settled marshy regions of the Lower Danube, about a shapeless apparition called the "weißen Alp."[1] It moved about in the villages in the shape of a white thread, stealing into the homes, waiting until nightfall and then placing itself on the open mouths of those sleeping, whereupon it grew into the shape of a monster. By next morning it had disappeared but the sleeper affected had gone mad. The "weiße Alp" had sucked out his soul and taken it off to dank gorges on the moor. Out of context this passage has more in common with the Gothic novel, with its strong overtones of the bizarre and the melodramatic. Storm manages to avoid these effects by relating his popular alien superstition to the somber, melancholy and ghostly associations of his Wild Moor in a manner reminiscent of *Wuthering Heights*. In popular tradition the bleakness and desolation of the moor have given rise to its being regarded as a region of

[1] "the white nightmare"

death and punishment and the gateway to hell, a halfway region of phantoms and ghosts. Specific evidence of this is when regional names like Wild Moor define a frontier between the land of the living and the land of the dead. Storm is quite specific in his associations when stating that though the "white Alp" was not known in these parts, many – especially the older villagers – have stories of meeting equally frightful apparitions in the mists at night or in the twilight on these moors.

Having staged his sinister scene, Storm proceeds to link his demonic (Alp) theme with his main characters as rapidly as possible. The Judge and his companion reach their destination – the village on the southern edge of the Moor – and the Judge pays a visit on the Sexton and his wife. The striking feature abut this scene is that though the Judge had come primarily to see the Sexton – the rather aggressively worldly-wise character responsible for Fehse's marriage – it is the Sexton's wife who steals the scene, scarcely allowing her husband to get a word in at all.

We are nevertheless given a clear idea of the sexton's personality and character in a few brief comments or fleeting snatches of his conversation. He is a compromising and compromised individual, who neglected the welfare of the young people, when he was in office, in favour of tending his land. Once retired, he looked after their interests much better – rather too well, in fact.

He is preoccupied with traditional, materialistic values, epitomized in the scene where the judge first meets him: he is loading dung. It is possible that he is intended as an unwittingly sinister character – he is, after all, responsible for the arrangement, which leads directly to Hinrich's death. Reasons for this view may be seen in Storm's allusion to his exchanging his 'Goldhaufen'[1] for 'ebene Erde".[2] Gold is frequently depicted by Storm in its traditional role in folklore, mythology and superstition as a magical and demonic element. It has a 'filthy lucre' touch about it in Storm's work, particularly when associated with hidden treasure: gold at the bottom of a well is the root cause of the tragedy in *In St. Jürgen*. In the case of the sexton, the exchange of his 'Goldhaufen' for land epitomizes the clash of demonic and territorial forces in a presageful way, for Margret is Hinrich's 'Goldhaufen', whom he 'betrays' and exchanges for the farm. When he decides he cannot live without her he exchanges part of the farm (the brown horse) for gold – and a plan, which Margret rejects. The gold ends up in the bottom of a well, just as Hinrich ends up in the bottom of a pond: a primitive form of revenge has been wreaked.

[1] pile of gold

[2] flat ground

The theme is linked very rapidly with the sexton's wife, whose first words are that there had already been an ill omen, when Hinrich and Margret were teenagers, just before their confirmation. Somebody had stolen her roses. The indications were that it was Margret but Hinrich had taken the punishment for it in school. Challenged by her husband that there are simply old school stories, the sexton's wife replies that it is a single thread running through their lives from then to now. The only time Storm uses the word *Faden* in the story is four paragraphs earlier in his reference to the *Alp* as "ein Ding, das einem weißen Faden gleicht…"[1] The link is certainly significant – a metaphor for the unhealthy hold Margret had exercised over Hinrich, right from childhood.

The sexton's wife continues with her story and supplies further details about both Margret and Hinrich, including the account of the early rivalry with Hans Ottsen – a rivalry which has continued down through to the present, now that the latter's father is dying, and can do little to prevent it. The most significant feature which emerges from her account is the fact that Hinrich Fehse had disappeared once before, after the *fracas* at the Confirmation Dance, when, ominously enough, once before, his approaches to Margret had been thwarted.

---

[1] something which is like a white thread

On that occasion he had stayed out not one night but two, a fact indicated by a somewhat poetic but ominously ambiguous phrase: "aber da hatte auch eine Eule gesessen"[1] (336) The whole village had set out in search of him with ladders and poles but a local lad had finally found him out on the moor, by a briny, black pond, "bei den Wasserkröten"[2] Gratopp has indicated how selective Storm is in his refernce to toads and how conscious he was of local myths which saw in toads the re-embodiments of the souls of the damned. They are usually associated in his work with the bewitched: Elsi, in *Ein Bekenntnis* a rather ghostly, otherworldly female, especially requests that no harm shall come to a toad in the garden, "Denn wer wisse, was hinter jenen goldenen Augen stecke".[3] There is no suggestion that Storm himself subscribed to these views but he had clearly saw in them an excellent and authentic vehicle for mirroring the more irrational and inexplicable ways of the human heart. Moreover, the places where people die in Storm's novellas are generally desolate, wet, ghostly and unwelcoming.

In this case, Hinrich has not died, though one could argue the case for a *Scheintod*.[4] The interesting point is that

[1] but an owl had something to do with that too

[2] with the water toads

[3] for who knows what hides behind those golden eyes

[4] suspended animation

60

Storm has set the whole scene *as if* he had died, clearly with premonitory intentions. There may even be anti-demonic allusions in the unusual name of Finkeljochim, the man who finds Hinrich. The sexton's wife, with a striking example of local superstition, rounds off the account.

When the doctor's efforts to cure the chilled and fevered Hinrich fail, the villagers resort to magic in prescribing three cups of camomile tea and passing over him "a few handfuls of church-yard earth." Earth, itself a healing element, was thought to be fortified in its powers by the bodies of the dead when it came from the church-yard. Its curative powers for a fever were well-known in North Germany. Storm may have taken the idea from one of Müllenhoff's *Sagen*, in which a woman seeks to turn away an evil spell by placing earth from the churchyard in her pocket. The fact that he intended the reference to carry more weight than a passing allusion is borne out by its repetition in the penultimate sentence of this novella. The sexton's wife has thus far occupied the centre of the stage and successfully prevented the Judge from conferring with her husband. She had nevertheless succeeded in "filling in the picture," and she is not without her worldly wisdom either.

The Judge proceeds now to the Fehses' farm. In doing so he passes the midwife's (and Margret's) house. Though it is spick and span he notes that an almost leafless elder hedge surrounds it. The twin allusions, where autumn equals death and the elder is the Tree of Death, are unmistakable examples of Storm's coding. It is quite relentlessly pursued for after Hinrich's material fortunes have been neatly mirrored in the state of the farm buildings and the pre-marriage state has been carefully balanced against the married one, Margret is re-introduced in a compromised way and against a sombre background – a pattern of black neatly linking all three themes, from the "schwarzen Lake"[1] and the "Dunkelwerden"[2] to "schwarzbraune Strohdach",[3] the "Schwarzwälder Uhr"[4] and the "schwarzes Kopftuch"[5] which Margret takes from her head. The sequence of 'black' allusions neatly leads up to a concentration of attention on this dark beauty's head. The final irony of the situation is neatly expressed by the inscription painted over one of the wall-beds and decorated with the forget-me-nots: "Ost un West, to Huss ist best."

With the cross-examination of Margret Glansky and the two Frau Fehses, the story enters its final phase. To Margret Glansky Storm attributes a reaction he had noted

[1] black brine

[2] "gathering darkness"

[3] the black brown thatched roof

[4] the Black forest clock

[5] the black head-scarf

with the girl in the original court case which gave rise to this novella: the predominant fear of official reprobation and the seeming indifference as to the fate of the man involved. The fear is succinctly expressed by Storm in the sentence: "Die Angst vor äußerlicher Verantwortlichkeit wegen einer vielleicht innerlichen Schuld…"[1] The girl is spirited and defiant, but cannot conceal the hatred which the village women bear her. Storm's technique of interrupting the cross-examination with the arrival of the Fehse women and briefly conferring with them before returning to the girl lends the scene a sense of pace and plastic realism in which the mutual antipathies have time to gel.

Margret's account of one of Hinrich's visits during his wife's sickness gives Storm the opportunity to include a piece of popular local necromancy – or more accurately, geomancy – the method of divination by means of points drawn at random on paper and then linked up to form a shape. It is significant that the book Hinrich uses for this purpose belongs to Margret's mother, for the gift of foretelling the future was until recently in this area ascribed to gypsies and midwives. Hinrich puts the question to the book of whether his sick wife will recover or not. He leaves abruptly and Margret checks the answer

[1] the fear of public responsibility for a secret guilt

in the book to find: "Tröstet die Seelen des Kranken und lasst alle Hoffnung fahren!"[1] But the wife recovers. Margret's account continues and relates how on the previous Sunday evening Hinrich had called after dark. It has been stormy ("auch heulte der Sturm um die Kirche") and cold. Hinrich had asked her to run away to America with him, showing her the gold he had received for his farm horses. The upshot of her refusal was that he had thrown the gold down the well and behaved very wildly, finally cursing her before storming off; Margret follows shortly after, to the Fehse farm and peers through the shutters. It was just as if Hinrich had seen her. Margret races home across the church-yard with the storm in her ears ("der alte Finkeljochim sass dann immer, die Toten schreien in den Gräbern,")[2] On this night Hinrich disappeared. Her account ends here and the Judge goes to the window, observing that in the pale light of dusk the trees stood black (sic) in the garden and the mists moved across the moor below like white veils.

The Judge now cross-examines the older Fehse woman – Hinrich's mother. Her account substantiated Margret's but emphasizes the bizarre and the blood-curdling. She had been preoccupied on that night with the fear that the

---

[1] comfort the souls of the sick and give up all hope

[2] old Finkeljochim always says the dead are crying out in the grave

pear-tree, planted by the barn at Hinrich's baptism would be blown down in the gale – a typical instance of Stormian symbolic prophecy. When she looks out of the window the tree is groaning and creaking against the barn. Then she thought she saw a shaggy, furry thing crawling along the wall beneath the window. A scratching on the shutter coincides with Hinrich's suddenly sitting bolt upright in bed, staring "mit ganz toten Augen nach dem Fenster zu".[1] The tension rises as the cattle create a commotion in the stalls and finally the bellowing of the bull is heard above the raging of the storm, as he tears at his chain. As Hinrich's eyes seem both "tot und glasig"[2] his mother sees what she thinks is an animal looking through the shutter with white pointed teeth and black eyes. The werewolf allusion is quite specific and the identification with Margret as well. The Judge's thoughts complete yet another identification of the demonic elements with Margret, when the latter's chalk-white complexion, red lips and lifeless appearance remind him of the *Alp* legend.

Storm takes pains to paralleled the legend in purely psychological terms. It is striking, for instance, that both Margret and Hinrich's mother refer in detail in their account to Hinrich's odd behaviour. When Margret

---

[1] staring at the window his eyes appearing dead

[2] dead and glassy

rejects his run-away proposal, Hinrich throws himself to the ground in a kind of fit and becomes "unsinnig".[1] His mother describes him as sitting up in bed "tot und glasig" and when he goes out to the barn in the storm he does so with a deep sigh and "wie taumelig". Perhaps the most accurate account of his condition is contained in the earlier confession to his mother when he had been out on horseback for five hours in the night. It is clearly a case of a man possessed – by the passion, which proves too strong for him and takes him to a watery grave. The *Alp* motif is now wound up in the rapid dénouement of the novella.

Appropriately enough and typical of his method, Storm announces Hinrich's death not through human communication but through sudden arrival into the room of the dead man's bedraggled dog, which had been missing with him – a brilliant stroke of realism, which Storm was to repeat in *Der Schimmelreiter* by announcing the Dyke Reeve's coming death through the medium of his ducks. As the dead farmer's body is brought into the barn, Margret rises from her chair "like a snake". With the public recognition that her son is dead, Fehse's mother tells Margret to go. She runs away with outstretched arms, as if there were something chasing her, soon disappearing

[1] "mad"

into the white mists, which had swept up from the moor. Thus Storm ties up his motif.

Caught between territorial and demonic imperatives, Hinrich Fehse falls victim to both for had the land question and traditional bourgeois obligation not obtained, he might never have married Ann-Marieken, the girl for whom he had no affection. The force of tradition is too strong for him and he succumbs rather than comply. His child alone has his affection and that dies within the year. Hans Ottsen married his widow and with the scattering of a few handfuls of churchyard soil by the sexton's wife, the rightful ordering of things is brought back to the community. Margret disappears into the anonymity of a neighbouring city. The demonic force is banished and the territorial imperative alone is restored to pre-eminence.

Draußen im Heidedorf is a fine psychological study of one man crushed by the "iron necessity" of a fixed, agrarian order of the society, on the other hand, and by an all-destroying passion, on the other. It is also an indictment of village *mores*, complacency and lack of understanding on the part of those who regard themselves as "weltklug".[1] Superstition and legend, magic and the black arts are present as still holding sway in what is essentially a

---

[1] worldly wise

pagan community. The theme was to become a prominent feature in the wider landscape of his writing.

The symbol of the land – and society's relationship to it – was to loom larger and larger in Storm's work from this point on. One thinks of its central role in *Renate*, where much of the tragedy stems from the fact that Renate's father, the Hofbauer, is particularly enlightened in his relationship to the land and the community cannot accept his success.

Then there is *Eekenhof*, where Herr Hennicke is prepared to destroy anything and anyone (including his own son), who stands between him and the increase of his property. Even much of *Die Söhne des Senators* hinges on the disputed garden and the question of its ownership. Implicit in both *Ein Fest auf Haderslevhuus* and *Ein Doppelgänger* is an agrarian order based on a lord and serf relationship, even though the former is set in mediaeval times and the latter in modern ones. Land plays, of course, a crucially symbolic role in *Der Schimmelreiter*, where the size of one's holding determines exactly which rank one may reach on the ladder of self-advancement. Hauke's father shows great foresight by purchasing land for his son, who reveals equal entrepreneurial wisdom by marrying into it.

Draußen im Heidedorf is a milestone is Storm's writing for several reasons. There is, first a marked development in style – a new tautness and control over digressive tendencies and a development of a crystalline, chiselled, honed and brilliantly evocative impressionistic method, which conveys the utmost through the barest of deft touches and the slightest of allusions. Second, though many of the earlier ingredients are there – the various and shifting points of view, the oblique (and not-so-oblique) references to superstitious behaviour and belief, the mythological and popular symbols, the economic lighting techniques – they are now all used less obtrusively, heavily disguised by the new, seemingly cool-headed and journalistic method of presentation. Third, there is a new scepticism – a profound questioning of the values of the 'old order' and serious doubts about its continuance. There is a tempering of the earlier optimism almost to the point of its total suppression. Coding is still very much in evidence and the kind of code words we have come to expect are still present, if anything more cleverly concealed and disguised.

We now move on to look closely at highly specialized techniques Storm employs, which offer us evidence in greater detail, in support of the general view of Storm's landscapes, outlined up to this point.

CHAPTER III

Temporal Considerations

While Storm's peculiar sensitivity to time has been noted by his critics, the wider dimensions have been largely overlooked, whether they be reflected in his hypersensitivity to the inevitable withering of all beauty or in his allergic reaction to the *Perpendikelschlag*[1] of the long-case clock or to the melancholy striking of a distant church bell. There is no doubt that this awareness plays a central role in Storm's novellas, colouring and distorting, stretching and telescoping, accelerating and retarding, in all, lending his material what Walter Brecht rightly calls *Perspektive*. Storm's view of time is a complex one, although

---

[1] perpendicular striking

unencumbered by the bric-à-brac of any contemporary formal philosophy. His time landscape is one of an all powerful, flowing continuum and as an ebb and flow in which an individual's life is but a brief flash of light and terms like past, present and future are strictly relative. Storm's time-mechanisms therefore merit closer attention not only as reflection of his time-response and *Weltanschauung*[1] but also as stylistic devices in his work. Let us now examine Storm's use of clocks, bells, bell-towers, day-night and seasonal counterpoles, and butterflies and moths, as part of his time-landscape

Storm sees timepieces as puny, fallible and suspect human attempts to catch time momentarily and measure it. Showing just how flexible a timepiece may be, Storm depicts Marthe's old clock as something which has never quite reconciled itself to 'modern times', striking irregularly at odd hours with all the whims and frailty of its elderly mistress. Conversely, in *Beim Vetter Christian*, Storm presents the old English 'Grandfather' clock meticulously chiming both hours and quarters. Although the effect is cyclical, as in *Under Milk Wood*, there is no space here for a Captain Cat reverie. At this stage the clock has a definite 'timekeeper' function, jogging Christian to bed and prodding him to school. It also plays a dual role

[1] world view

as a protector – shielding him by its loud ticking from the prying Tante Karoline. The church clock assumes a similar role at one in the morning, as does Christian's room bell later that day.

All this time we are aware of Storm using the clock or bell as a retarding device, slowly marking time and guarding privacy, gradually building up interest to the very precipitate dénouement of the story. With Vetter Christian's marriage his whole time-experience is changed: gone is the gentle pace of his bachelor days, gone also is his privacy. His time-experience is peremptorily accelerated, a point which Storm makes quite explicit in the final paragraphs with phrases like "Und die Stunden flogen"[1] and "Vier Jahre sind seitdem verflossen."[2] The acceleration is clearly extended to his character for in the brief space of four years the middle-aged bachelor becomes *pater familias*, a candidate for the board of the *Volksbank* and is for his wife's tastes "gar zu regsam."[3] In all, Storm plods slowly through the space of approximately nine months for most of his tale, only to speed through four years in the penultimate paragraph! This light vein of irony runs right through the story, not only in instances such as Tante Karoline's chagrin in precipitating the marriage while

[1] and the hours flew by

[2] four years have passed by since then

[3] far too active

trying to achieve exactly the opposite but particularly in this oscillating treatment of time. It is noteworthy that Storm returns to the sober, measured time of the earlier part of the story in his final paragraph: "Aber es ist acht Uhr! As much as to say, 'all this marrying business temporarily went to his head but now we're back on the rails again.' By this means he preserves both a cyclical and an ebb-and-flow time impression, which lends the story an illusion of balance even though the time-emphasis has been on one of disproportion.

A further example of Storm's technique of retarding/ accelerating time may be seen in *Drüben am Markt* in the special emphasis made on 'old' versus 'new' time. The old glass-cased mantel clock has not been wound up for twenty-five years – a mirror to the general self neglect of its owner – but it does tick loudly and keep time "wie vor füfundzwanzig Jahren," when the Doctor does wind it up. Its crime is that it belongs to the old order so it is replaced by a shiny, new, metallic one. The new clock, it turns out, goes fast, echoing the impetuosity of its owner, and gaining three hours in a week. The acceleration of the clock mirrors the Doctor's hasty assumptions that Mamsell Sophie will agree to marry him. In his allusion to Clotho, the spinning Goddess of Fate depicted in porcelain on top of the new clock, there are, conceivably, intentionally sinister undertones, in the sense that the three Goddesses of Fate are regarded on the one hand as the impartial representatives of the government of the world, and on the other sometimes men. It is exactly the type of allusion of which Storm was fond and fits the Doctor's case precisely.

To appreciate the multiple role clocks and bells play in Storm's novellas one must first come to terms with their multiple role. As reminder mechanisms they often intrude on and deflect the thoughts of his characters, prompting them to action and intervening in the plot, as it were. In the early novellas up to *Drüben am Markt* (1860) they figure largely as 'etwas lebendig'[1], - as harmless companions of man and 'conversationalists' for the lonely. From *Veronika* (1861) on, however, they take on a sinister colour, which varies considerably in intensity. In *Veronika* the association of bells and death is heavily underscored. In *In St. Jürgen* (1867), whereas most commentators have singled out the swallow motif for special attention, the bell motif is also significant and has specifically sinister connotations. It is true that the swallow motif plays a central role thematically and with its cyclical function serves as a kind of fate-chorus to the narrative. The birds' seasonal comings and goings help to counterpoint not only the hopes and longings but also the frustrations and ultimate

---

[1] slightly lively

misery of the two main characters. But reaction to this motif has been varied. Common to all commentaries, however, is the fact that the bell imagery appears to have escaped attention. Bell images out number swallow images in *In St. Jürgen* by nearly two to one. Since incidence is almost invariably a reliable pointer in Storm to motif and structure, the bell imagery deserves closer attention.

The church clock and its bell are an integral part of an image cluster, which comprises swallows, tower and bell. Agnes' first concrete evidence of something seriously amiss with her father occurs pointedly as the church clock strikes midnight. This scene contains certain stock Stormian images for a demonic setting: midnight, brilliant (full?) moon shining on elder hedge with its leafless (lifeless?) branches, fiery Faustian red glow in the well-shaft, bushes round about glowing with golden fire and the explicit superstition of the little grey man sitting at the bottom of the well with a candle. Her father's bankruptcy follows quickly and bell imagery is at the heart of his disgrace for the public announcement is accompanied by the ringing of the *Schandglocke*.[1]

The space Storm gives to the devious steps Agnes takes to prevent her father from hearing the bell is fair indication of the depth of its role in the story. It is an association of

[1] disgrace bell

warnings, ignominy and destruction from this point on. This initial calamity scene is neatly concluded with the 'chorus' appearance of the swallows at Agnes' window. The narrator suggests they are congratulating her on the paying off of her father's debts but in fact they remind her that the price has been her happiness, lost in the south, whence the birds have come.

The church tower plays an important role in the image cluster as is clearly demonstrated in the next scene. Unbeknown to Harre, the church tower had been pulled down forty years previously. It had a special psychological significance for him as the final parting-place from Agnes. The broken-down tower mirrors Agnes' broken hopes and Harre's broken promise. The novella is neatly framed by the image of the tower *in the memory* of the two main characters: Agnes and Harre. The association is an unhappy one for both of them – grief at the loss of what might have been – and though the tower is torn down, the swallows are an ever-recurring annual reminder of it. Further ironies are associated with it: the ritual welcoming of the swallows in spring by the tower-keeper on his horn, Harre's distaste for the old tower clock "carrying on its work in this solitude" and the stressing of spring and sunshine around it, which only increases its traumatic role in Harre's memory. The ironic contrasts involved are typically Stormian – Spring *Wanderlust* juxtaposed with an underlying sense of betrayal; the *Unendlichkeit des Raumes*[1] broken only by the church spire; the total solitude interrupted only by the rattling of the great clock, radiant, blossoming present juxtaposed with a dim and dark future. Overall is a metaphysical sense of timelessness, suddenly brought down to earth by the insistent tolling of the quarter-hour bell. The 'chorus' reappears and stresses the basic theme: "Vergiß das Wiederkommen nicht![2] The image cluster reappears in the middle of the next scene in stark proportions. Harre is giving an account of his experiences working in the south, often overcome with homesickness in the middle of his work.

Storm treads perilously close to banal sentimentality with touches like the *Vergißmeinnicht*-blue of Agnes' dress but manages to subsume such touches in the larger dream-sequence, tempered as it is by the sinister images of threatening black tower, autumnal storm and the plangent tolling of the heavy bells – a well-known warning signal in the region. The spring-versus-autumn clash in this sequence echoes the fundamental motif of hope versus destruction running through this novella and also indicates a symbolic time manipulation of the seasons. The close links between the images of tower, swallows and bell

---

[1] the infinity of space

[2] Don't forget the return

are finally demonstrated in the dénouement of this tale, where the old Spökenkieker[1] – one of Storm's singularly demonic figures – points to the swallows actually gathering on the bell itself on the roof of the Stift, prior to migration. Storm is fond of using migrating birds as a metaphor for the passing of time. Here he is only intensifying the metaphor for the tower itself is linked closely to the passing of time. The tower and bell motif assumes metaphysical proportions. Though not as consciously philosophical as John Donne's:

> …any man's *death* diminishes *me*,
> because I am involved in *Mankind*;

And therefore never send to know for whom the *bell* tolls; it tolls for *thee*…

For Storm in no way allows Harre to stress his oneness with his fellow man, there is nevertheless the implication that the bell tolling for Agnes is also tolling for Harre. The schism within Harre is epitomized by his love-hate relationship with the tower, the clock and the swallows.

Further clock and time techniques may be seen to advantage in *Viola Tricolor*. Here the opening paragraph is dominated by the flowing of time from its beginnings through to eternity. One of Ines' major psychological

---

[1] ghost watcher

79

hurdles is to overcome her fear that her husband's first marriage can only be dissolved by the death of both partners – and what if the first one is the only true wife on into eternity? And her own child a bastard? The problem turns into a nightmare with suicidal proportions only to be resolved by the cathartic experience Ines has in the new garden, when she mistakes Nero the Newfoundland dog for large attacking Hounds of Hell and is 'rescued' by her husband. The whole problem – that of temporary mental darkness and hallucinations is cleverly mirrored in the light imagery of the story. Storm was a master at working in the twilight zone where reality shades off into unreality – one thinks of the high proportion of twilight and specifically night scenes in his work and the clever use of moonlight in *Der Schimmelreiter*. In *Viola tricolor*, Ines' mental journey from suicidal dark anguish through to the daylight of resolution is paralleled by the fact that the tale moves from moonlight into sunlight only in the penultimate paragraph. It is altogether a twilight tale of ghostly moonlight and shadows. The night-day resolution is, of course, also a time-sequence in which time has been symbolically distorted – it has been a very long night leading to the day. The English clock in the introduction plays an important role in epitomizing the flow of this time process. As an antique it points back to the past beyond reminiscence; its pendulum measures the present and as a metaphor of continuity it points into the (family) future.

Yet another time-image in *Viola tricolor* is to be seen in the two gardens and in Storm's highly subjective treatment of them. His technique of treating time with the utmost flexibility adds new dimensions to what might otherwise be a banal theme. He achieves this by applying his technique of *Dämonisierung*[1] to the old garden, thereby focussing attention on it dramatically. Not only is it specifically a *Garten der Vergangenheit*[2] and a tomb, it is also a wilderness surrounded by a high wall, where the sole building lies in ruins, the roses are *verdorrt*,[3] the birds (a pair of swallows and a robin) have possibly dubious associations, and passing reference to a large night-moth reveals one of Storm's more oblique death-mages. A final association with the black Tree of Death can leave us in no doubt about Storm's intentions. The old garden joins other sepulchral arenas in Storm's work, like the island of Jeverssand in *Der Schimmelreiter*, which exert a baleful demonic influence on the whole story. The crisis in the story is seen to stem from Rudolf's unhealthy worship of the dead past. The old garden has become a symbol of Rudolf's incapacity to give up the all-powerful memory of

[1] demonization

[2] garden of the past

[3] dried up

81

his first wife. She is thus seen to be exerting even in death a fateful influence on both the present and the future. A similar technique may be seen in *Bahnwärter Thiel*, where the signalman turns his signal-box into a shrine to his first wife, thereby jeopardizing his second marriage. In Rudolf's case the shrine is composed both of the old garden and his study; the two areas are carefully linked together, for the study is the sole vantage point in the house from which to view the old garden. Ines becomes aware of this situation and taxes Rudolf with it. The cultivated shadow of the past is choking life in the present. Even birdsong is seen as raising "trügerische(n) Hoffnungen".[1] With the safe birth of the child and the recovery of its mother the garden time-sequence undergoes a change. Its derelict, dead aspect is transformed. The scene moves from moonlight into sunlight. A way has been cut through to the gateway, the birds are singing, creepers are in blossom, the white gravel path now shines in the sun, the conifers are dark green instead of black, bees hum and swallows have nested in the ruined *Gartenhaus*. In a transformation worthy of Wilde's *Selfish giant*, the garden of death has suddenly become a garden of life. A decision is now taken to accept life (and the present) and the children's voices are an unmistakable pointer to the future: "…behütet von

[1] misleading hopes

der alten Dienerin, hielt die fröhliche Zukunft des Hauses ihren Einzug in den Garten der Vergangenheit".[1] Storm has used the old garden to great effect, holding it up as a mirror and metaphor to the psychological state of his lead characters, stretching the time-sequence to embrace on the one hand forgotten past and on the other, pointers to eternity. One final aspect of this technique remains to be considered. In depicting his *Garten der Vergangenheit* predominantly by moonlight and ultimately in the sun, Storm is not simply making the point that day inevitably follows night. In polarizing moonlight and sunlight he effectively adds several new dimensions to his story. For the moonlight associations of madness, hallucinations, dreams, death, hopelessness and the demonic to be found in the garden exactly parallel Ines' mental crisis, for each of these themes is struck in the night excursion scene. Conversely, Storm associates clarity, recovery, freshness, health and hope in the future directly with the change in the garden to sunshine and birdsong.

As a variation on the theme of the clock as a subjective and flexible measuring device, Storm's treatment of the Black Forest cuckoo-clock in *Waldwinkel* is particularly illuminating. We have seen how the Grandfather clock dominated the introduction to *Viola tricolor*, measuring

---

[1] watched over by the old servant

time at a regular, controlled rate, emphasizing both continuity, established routine and the continued existence of the old regime, showing the house thoroughly in the grip of the (choking) past, in effect, retarding the time-impression. As the story progresses this image of the clock recedes and disappears by the time that Rudolf and Ines have struggled through to a new time-response. The cuckoo-clock in *Waldwinkel* plays a dual role, both pacing the story from first to last and symbolically underscoring its central irony. It is first depicted as a pretty decoration, neatly measuring the time. As the dramatic tension increases so does the striking of the clock, which is linked with increasingly ominous associations. This is just the opposite process from the 'Grandfather' in *Viola tricolor*, which helped to retard the impression of time. Here we have a clear-cut case of acceleration of time as a stylistic device, through repeated emphasis on a clock's striking. Unobtrusive as it is, it is nonetheless effective.

The clock's second role is emblematic. In a novella which is saturated with bird imagery, the wide range of bird reference, which includes the heavily symbolic falcon motif, serves as an excellent cover for the man-made bird in the Black Forest clock. As early as *Immensee* Storm had demonstrated how scrupulous he is in his use of bird imagery, particularly with reference to the cuckoo. Almost invariably he uses it in conjunction with its traditional association with cuckolding. There is no reason to think he is not using the same association in *Waldwinkel* – and every reason to think he is. For the story, if nothing else, is a story of cuckolding. That is not to say that Storm makes the cuckoo's role an obvious one. It is brilliantly disguised and merges into the general décor and furnishings of the manor-house so unobtrusively as to belie its real function. The cuckoo-clock in many ways epitomizes the poetic and the realistic in Storm's writing. As a part of the furnishings it is utterly convincing at its surface level. At its symbolic level it mirrors the central idea of this novella. In this process, the cuckoo, with the agitated flapping of its wings, plays both a premonitory role as well as that of ironic commentator. It is noteworthy that it is not confined to the 'real' world of the senses but also carries over into the 'unreal' world of unconsciousness. On the bird's two, final appearances Richard is asleep and yet it appears to get its message through to him, for it is after he has restlessly 'listened' to it striking through the night that his bad dreams begin and he awakes to find his guard-dog shot and his mistress abducted. Other examples of Storm's use of clocks and bells as premonitory devices may be found in *Eekenhof*, where the manor-house clock is specifically *Unheil drohend*[1] and a constant reminder of

[1] threatening misfortune

Herr Hennicke's crimes; in *Die Armesünderglocke,* where there is a specific association of the tolling bell accompanying the criminal to his execution, in *Hans und Heinz Kirch,* where the recollected ringing of the *Bürgerglocke* to ring the curfew in for young people has premonitory significance for Heinz Kirch. In *Carsten Curator* clocks are associated with mortality and presentiments of evil. The death association of the Grandfather clock mentioned early in the story is made quite specific: it houses the hobbyhorse of the boy snatched away by smallpox. The clock is depicted as feelinglessly attempting to measure 'fleeting time', now as then, a constant reminder of man's mortality. As evidence of his explicitly shaky business enterprises in Hamburg, Heinrich holds up his expensive gold watch and chain for Anna to view. The gesture is a bitterly ironic one on Storm's part, since much of the tragedy hinges on gold and its fatal attractions for both father and son. The *goldene Uhr* is so-called evidence of successful wheeler-dealing, "von denen Heinrich sich goldene Berge versprochen hatte".[1] Add to this the heavily sinister role that gold in any quantity plays in Storm's work generally, and time then takes on demonic undertones. Later in the same novella on separate occasions Anna counts the strikes of the church clock while waiting for her inebriated husband to return

---

[1] from which Heinrich had promised himself mountains of gold

home and the sympathetic night watchman moves on out of distance before making his call.

In concluding the discussion of Storm's use of time-mechanisms it should be noted that Storm is capable on occasion of using them as a metaphor of happiness. The tolling of the bells in *Zur Chronik von Grieshuus* to celebrate peace is a case in point. He is even capable of blending the sinister with the joyful with such mechanisms. In *Schweigen* Storm relieves the almost unbearable tension of the forester about to commit suicide by sounding a distant bell just as the forester is reaching for his gun. By counting the strokes of the bell the forester realises his wife must have read his explanatory suicide note and so the terrible 'silence' must be over. Here, the technique is contrived, to say the least, but it is perhaps less obvious than I have made it sound for it is part of a pattern of allusions in an atmosphere which is decidedly charged and heavy: as the suicidal act is imminent there is quick, successive reference to robins and a bluetit, fading lilies, *Schwarzbrotschnitte*,[1] and yellow leaves falling from the trees – a favourite Stormian image for decay and lifelessness. But with the striking of the bell the scene is transformed. Here we have a clear-cut case of a timely and essentially benevolent bell – a rarity in Storm's prose.

[1] blackbread slices

There is something to be said for the argument that Storm's inordinate sensitivity to the phenomenon of time is expressed ultimately in terms of its smallest units. In a penetrating essay on the problem of time in Storm, Karl Friedrich Boll suggests Ernst Jünger's 'hourglass' view of time, as opposed to that measured by mechanisms, reflects a view of time which "runs down, elapses and trickles away." Storm would like to catch each grain of sand as it goes through – and cherish it. Though time is sometimes conquered by the act of remembering, remembering may have the opposite effect. Storm's time-response is deeply imbued with irony for time and the grim reaper are frequently synonymous. His use of irony with regard to his time-mechanisms extends to other seemingly innocuous objects, notably, butterflies and birds.

Butterflies and moths – like the rose – epitomise for Storm one of his major metaphysical problems: what kind of a being could permit the growth of such a short-lived and intense beauty – a beauty compromised by the knowledge that time would destroy it so swiftly? It is almost a seventeenth century heightened awareness of the ineluctable and of the 'sudden death' nature of existence – a spinning-coin view of the world: on one side the smiling face of fortune, on the other, the hideous, toothless grin of the skeleton. But whereas the rose frequently becomes a private hieroglyph for death in Storm's work, butterflies and moths carry their own traditional burden of death and the macabre, as Storm clearly well knew. They are favourite death-images of his in both verse and prose and once again, we meet that characteristic amalgam of science and myth, which I have already suggested is central to virtually all of his work. As a youth Storm was an energetic lepidopterist, mounting his collection of butterflies and moths in three glass cases on the wall. Much of the episode 'Im Schloßgarten' in the novella *Auf der Universität* – and particularly that section dealing with butterfly collecting – is patently autobiographical. Storm described the scene later as "aus meiner innersten Jugend heraus geschrieben."[1] He takes great care with the naming of his butterflies and moths; their Latin names sometimes even appear in the text.

There appear to be no overt references in Storm's letters – or, for that matter, in his novellas – to a specific knowledge of the mythological associations of butterflies and moths. It would be unusual if there were. There is, however, overwhelming internal evidence to show that Storm was patently aware of their function in mythology and superstition, and that in this respect he was in the mainstream of mythological tradition. As early as the Etruscans, butterflies and moths featured as

---

[1] written from my deepest, innermost youth

the paramount personifications of the soul. They were frequently depicted on glyptographs and sarcophagi immediately above a skull. The tradition of the butterfly as an embodiment of the soul has survived into modern times both among civilized and primitive peoples. Goethe makes use of the tradition in the second part of Faust. In Germanic mythology butterflies have an ambivalent role. They are either good omens – or (predominantly) evil ones, with strong associations with witches and the devil. In Friesland moths are regarded by the superstitious as witches. The multiple sinister functions of butterflies and moths in Germanic tradition include those of morbific agent (*Krankheitsdämon*), oracular creature (good balances roughly with bad), and vegetation demon. Altogether, as embodiment of the soul, dead ancestors, children's souls, elves and witches – as a witch it steals milk, cream and butter, as the producer of *Alpdruck*, the carrier of the plague, fevers and mental disorders, and as an oracle of mixed blessing, the butterfly (and moth) plays a heavily sinister role in the landscape of mythology.

If one looks at the butterfly panoramically in Storm's work, the influence of this kind of thinking is marked. There is the 'dunkler Schmetterling'[1] of the poem 'Tiefe

---

[1] the dark butterfly

Schatten"[1] – that cycle of poems written on the death of Constanze; then there is the 'Nachtschmetterling-Grab'[2] association in *Viola tricolor,* the night-moth in *Ein grünes Blatt,* as Gabriel leaves for the battle-front, the "zwei dunkle Schmetterlinge" in front of the sinister forest tavern in *Auf der Universität.* There is the dead Juliane in *Carsten Curator,* described as "ein fremder Schmetterling". There is Kuno, the sickly boy marked out for death in *Im Schloß,* who is preoccupied with butterflies and bumble-bees – themselves ominous hieroglyphs. Franz, the sculptor in *Psyche,* alludes to the butterfly-death association. There are the night-moths, which introduce the final death-scene in *Auf dem Staatshof,* there is a barn-owl-night-moth association in *Im Nachbarhause Links.* Closely linked with the Undine-figure of Elsi in *Ein Bekenntnis* is the peacock butterfly, which takes a daily ride in her blond hair. There are the 'Abendschmetterling' and the 'Dämmrungsfalter' of that most demonic of Storm's poems – 'Gartenspuk'. Pride of place, however, for the most macabre use of this particular *memento mori* must go to the reference Storm's makes in *Ein Doppelgänger* to the *Totenkopf* or Death's-head moth. It occurs in the death-scene of John Hansen, who has had the misfortune to fall down an open well-shaft in the fields.

---

[1] Deep shadows

[2] night butterfly grave

His shouts for help go unheard by a fourteen year old boy, who is out in the fields with his butterfly-net, in search of a *Totenkopf.* Shortly afterwards, Hansen's body provides the carrion for an unusually large falcon: gruesome stuff! Yet Storm was not entirely alone in this particular field. Theodor Fontane makes similar macabre use of the butterfly in *Unwiederbringlich*, where it turns up as the Erichsen family's monogram on the family tombstones. Detlev von Liliencron was also clearly conversant with butterfly mythology for explicit death associations with the butterfly run through his poem 'Schmetterlinge'. They also occur in his poems 'An der Grenze' and 'Una ex hisce morietis'. Hermann Löns alludes to the death and soul associations in *Der Wehrwolf.*

Having said that, it should be noted that Storm is capable of using butterflies for quite different purposes – as images of summer (beautiful evanescence) or *Sommermüdigkeit*[1] – see the blue arguses in *Ein grünes Blatt* – or longing, and even as an image of love. The lovelorn doctor in *Drüben am Markt* sadly and enviously watches the pairing of the *Brennesselfalter.* Fritz Basch chases a brimstone-butterfly or even a peacock butterfly in *Bötjer Basch* addressing it as 'Sommervagel'. Most of these semipositive associations are to be found in *Auf der*

---

[1] summer tiredness

Universität, underscoring the butterfly's multiple role in Storm's work. He devotes virtually the whole of the scene 'Im Schloßgarten' to a butterfly chase. Philipp, the youthful narrator, is in love with Lore Beauregard, the French tailor's daughter. But his love goes unheeded. His 'hunt' for Lore is mirrored in this chase after a very special kind of butterfly. Philipp is a butterfly collector and Storm lists names like 'Argusfalter', 'Trauermantel', 'Zitronenfalter', 'Kressweißling' and 'Leineule' not simply as evidence of entomological good faith and the new realism but also with prophetic intent – playing upon our suspicions with names like 'Trauermantel'. The hunt, in this case, is for the 'Brombeerfalter'. Here, the identifications with Lore is unequivocal: She had been described earlier as having a "bräunliche Hautfarbe" and the butterfly is described as "dieses schöne olivenbraune Sommervögelchen",[1] and, like Lore, is "eine Seltenheit".[2] What begins in this scene as an essentially practical enterprise develops into a reverie of Romantic proportions. Many of the stock images are there: the secret place reached only through obstructions *(Hagedornhecken),*[3] the special tree or 'Wunderbaum' ("Wie ein Wunder stand er da in dieser Einsamkieit"),the humming of bees, the solitude, the singing of the lark,

[1] this beautiful olive brown little summerbird

[2] a rarity

[3] hawthorn hedges

the heavy 'cloud' of scent. The pattern of Stormian stereotypes is unmistakable and highly characteristic of his *Stimmungskunst*. It is capped by the bucolic reveries of the youth – himself the shepherd, Lore the Shepherdess – "Allein auf der Welt". The pervading theme is that of longing, the atmosphere and technique markedly that of *Taugenichts* – including the final gesture, when he throws away his butterfly net forever. Some would argue that it is very much the 'Kitsch' part of Storm's 'Kunst'. Yet the butterfly imagery is nonetheless effective and epitomizes Lore's all-too-brief existence.

Storm's use of the butterfly or moth is therefore very consistent with his use of other images drawn from nature, particularly when compared with those images which have traditional symbolic significance in mythology, i.e., with plants and trees, with exotic animals and particularly with birds. His knowledge of the particular mythological associations is clearly more extensive than hitherto was believed to be the case. He is well aware of the butterfly's traditional associations with death, the soul and sickness, with children's rhymes and sunny summer days, with love and longing. But a heavy preponderance of his references to butterflies associates the themes of beauty and death – and evanescence. We have seen above how they relate with clocks and bells directly to his time-experience but alone they constitute an extraordinary entomological landscape.

CHAPTER IV
The Landscape of Birds

Nowhere else in Storm's oeuvre do we meet Storm's characteristic bifocal view of nature more clearly than in his treatment of birds. Here we meet at one and the same time the highly skilled ornithologist and the consummate mythologist working harmoniously in tandem. The vast majority of his ornithological landscapes are peppered with an extraordinary range of bird species (over eighty), the behavioural aspects of which are treated with great care and scientific accuracy. This alone places him in the top three of all European writers. Not only do they provide us with a useful index of his relation to Poetic Realism but they also illuminate in a way unlike any of his other symbols that special irony, paradox and ambivalence which lies at the core of all his work. Compounded with the scientific accuracy are the many mythological allusions concealed, in weather, coloration, sound and erratic behaviour all reflected in the major characters in a specific novella. Birds are scattered through his verse, his Märchen, almost all of the novellas and much of his private correspondence. On the surface they appear to be incidentals and slightly eccentric marginalia of only passing merit, for their hidden symbolism is cleverly concealed at sub-surface level. Such is the unique nature of this extraordinary literary technique, whereby Storm's synthesis of detailed science and sinister superstition can pass by the reader almost unnoticed, without disturbing the sensuous nature of a scene in the landscape, so that signs may be seen pointing ahead to the Naturalists. It might be described as the confrontation of the bird with the demon in Storm's muse. It is as well to consider at this point some of the people and influences that came to bear in developing Storm the natural scientist. His interest in birds must have come by osmosis since he deferred all his life to his father's profound interest in ornithology.

It is clear that Storm was well versed in bird mythology. There are a half dozen explicit references in Storm's work to birdlore: they are to be found in allusions to the tawny owl as a *Totenvogel*,[1] to owls hooting on a rooftop prior to the death of an occupant of the house, to the lapwing as a damned soul, to the raven as a bird of wisdom, to the swallow as a herald of spring, and especially in Storm's references to the nightingale – as we shall see below.

Storm's birds conveniently divide into two basic groups. First, there are the harbingers of spring and emblems of love, which generally evoke feelings of freedom, joy and happiness – the benevolent birds. Among these would be the nightingale, the lark, the swallow, the stork and the bullfinch. The second group, which is by far the larger, comprises the birds of ill omen, that is, the birds of prey and the predators. These would include vultures, eagles, ospreys, kites, harriers, hawks, falcons, owls, ravens and rooks, crows, jays, magpies, jackdaws and gulls, together with other birds of ominous reputations, colour or cry like lapwings, blackbirds, starlings, curlews, plovers, waders – or those with seemingly vicious habits, like the shrike or butcher-bird. Generally speaking, Storm is much more successful in his exploitation of the second group, for several reasons. The nightingale and the lark had already established themselves as relatively fixed literary conventions. They had been widely used as such by Storm's contemporaries – by Eichendorff in particular.

---

[1] bird of death

As conventions their use was circumscribed and variation could only be achieved by treating them ironically, as Storm does frequently. As Storm's novellas turn to blacker themes with more tragic outcomes, images connotating happiness, freedom and joy tend to become superfluous, except for purposes of ironic contrast or of stressing the idea of transience. And so, as one might expect, Storm uses both lark and nightingale very sparingly in the later novellas. Sinister birds of ill omen reflect more accurately – and with greater variety, since there are more of them! – the pessimistic *Weltanschauung*[1] Storm is at pains to project in his novellas. Since tragic themes of violent death predominate in the later novellas, it is not surprising that Storm becomes preoccupied with the use of birds whose sudden appearance or strange behaviour traditionally prognosticate evil in general and death in particular. So consistent is Storm in his use of birds as sinister hieroglyphs that the watchful reader can almost invariably orientate himself in Storm's tragic landscapes by using them as markers.

Storm's encyclopaedic knowledge of bird folklore and superstition allows him to pick and choose from either group, according to the needs of landscape, plot and character. A close reading of each novella will disclose which

[1] worldview

group is surfacing and for what purpose. Sometimes one group like the swallows in 'The Swallows of St. George' will emerge beneficially only to be linked ironically with the final tragedy. Conversely, the eagle association with Herr Hennicke, the main character in 'Grieshuus: the Chronicle of a Family', is subsumed from the murderous and predatory nature of his first appearance to his transformation as a reformed and benevolent character at the end.

As one explores the landscape of Storm's birds one becomes aware that Storm is no dabbler, no dilettante, dipping into a collection, one here, one there, for he clearly sees them as part of a greater artistic whole. The conclusion is inescapable that they represent a major controlling force in his narratives – introducing, evoking, clarifying, transforming and epitomizing, out of which character, plot, scene and events flow. We begin therefore to appreciate Storm's bigger picture, just as the painter includes punts, barges and horses not as addenda but as crucial to the comprehension of the painting as a whole. This is not to ignore the many tensions between landscape and character, to be seen no more distinctly than in the motif of the wolves in '*Grieshuus*'.

The whole question of the accuracy of Storm's bird nomenclature is very revealing. I have shown how Storm's range of bird references is prodigious and far in excess of his contemporaries. He goes far beyond the norms of Poetic Realism, yet perhaps intuitively, not far enough to be regarded as 'the naturalist as poet'. Storm is essentially the creative artist, with one eye always on scientific fact. He is a practical and self taught observer – the archetypal poet-naturalist. Other important considerations are visible in so far as Storm is not only acutely aware of birds as colour phenomena, he is also superbly aware of the sounds birds make and he is a master in orchestrating these sounds emblematically in his work. The sounds birds make tend to clarify their role in the story – the raven's croak or the seagull's scream emphasize their threatening or warning role; the lark's singing can mirror the feelings of elation and high spirits and the nightingale talks of love. At least they will croak, mew or sing correctly!

Much of the paradox of life for Storm is contained in his poem *Käuzlein* (little owl), in which he parodies the antithetical role of the owl and the nightingale, traditional representatives of the worlds of death and love, paralleling a similar conflict portrayed by the anonymous author of "The Owl and the Nightingale" some six hundred years earlier. Storm's poem, written in 1843, serves as a useful pointer to Storm's later manipulation of birds.

Of all birds in literature the nightingale holds a position of unquestioned pre-eminence. More has been written to or about this bird than to any other bird in literature. As such it is a major literary convention. But it is a convention, which has undergone several metamorphoses since the days of classical Greece and Rome. In Greece and Rome the bird was generally highly prized for its singing but it was also associated in a fable by Ovid with tragedy and lament. It has become known as the legend of Philomela.

The twin strands of nightingale tradition – the murderous one of Ovid and the careless rapture of Pliny – appear to find a home in English and German literature respectively. We are clearly dealing with the existence of the common, traditional use of the nightingale as a symbol. It appears to be tied in inextricably with the doctrine of courtly love. The hidden meaning is derived from the *act* of listening to the bird singing, for the bird stands for two things which the lovelorn singer can no longer do: it can still sing and it can love without hindrance.

There is much evidence to show that Storm was conversant with this and most other literary legends associated with the nightingale, for this bird ranges through his early work with considerable mobility. It is only in the later, more sombre works that it disappears from view. In *Hinzelmeier*, a tale heady with the symbolism of roses and nightingales, drawn frequently from Romantic convention, Storm embodies in Hinzelmeier's song a direct allusion to the bird's song and roses springing up. Most of the nightingale literary conventions are to be found in

Heine, however. He strikes the theme of *Liebesschmerz* (lover's grief), the coming of spring in *Gekommen ist der Mai,* the irony of their beautiful singing. The theme of love occurs 'in *Der Tod, das ist die kühle Nacht,* of lament (*Klagelieder*) in *Altes Lied,* the theme of the rose as bride of the nightingale – *Die mondscheingefütterte Nachtigallbraut:* – in *Der Gesang der Okeaniden,* and in *Der Schmetterling (butterfly) ist in die Rose verliebt.* He refers to 'Philomele' in *die schönen Augen der Frühlingsnacht* and gives a variant of the rose bursting forth in *Im Anfang war die Nachtigall.*

Pliny's Natural History, regarded as a scientific source-book in the Middle Ages, lists many of these associations: the nightingale's ceaseless singing as the buds swell, the idea of song-contests between birds, in which the loser may die from exhaustion and loss of breath and the nightingale as essentially a bird of spring. Storm alludes to the "sing-ing-itself-to-death" legend in *Ein Fest auf Haderslevhuus* where the nightingale always sings as each love-scene reaches its climax. But in one scene Dagmar makes this curious observation, while the nightingale is singing: "She's dying. Oh can one die of love?" The classical source is unmistakable. Equally strong is the association with *Minnesang,* for the whole of this scene is dominated, as is much of this novella – by the symbol of the nightingale.

Although one can scarcely talk of a true bird-motif in *Ein Fest auf Haderslevhuus,* for the nightingale first appears halfway through this novella, the latter half is saturated with its imagery and symbolic overtones. Rolf underscores the nightingale-rose-passionate love theme linking it with white roses. In *Auf der Universität* the nightingale is referred to as an unequivocal harbinger of spring and in *Von Jenseit des Meeres* as an unmistakable symbol of love with a specific rose-nightingale association.

With *Aquis submersus*, however, the melancholy – if not tragic – associations of the nightingale with seduction and death (Philomela) are consistently underscored. Johannes, fleeing from the Junker Wulf's hounds, orientates himself in the woods by the nightingales' singing. They are clear seductive pointers leading him to his one, fatal night of love, just as they are for Rolf Lembeck, leading him to Dagmar in *Ein Fest auf Haderslevhuus*. The night of love shared by Johannes and Katharina is also heralded by the singing of nightingales in the garden below. The scene is heavily *stimmungsvoll* (atmospheric) with the typical image-cluster of birdsong, the burbling of water, moonshine, the heavy scent of flowers through the window and lightning-flashes in the distance. Storm is clearly exploiting the traditional motif of loss of virginity, which has attached itself to the nightingale at various times, for the loss of Katharina's virginity at this point, as Johannes enters the *Venusberg,* constitutes the *Wendepunkt* (turning point) of the story. From then on it accelerates to its tragic end. The Philomela association is therefore singularly relevant. As an early forewarning of Bas Ursel's hostility to the love-match (for it is she who betrays it), Storm emphasizes her antipathy for nightingales – the birds of love.

But there are further associations demonstrably connected with the nightingale, which indicate the range of Storm's familiarity with nightingale literary lore. In his "Song of the Nightingale", John Lydgate had already linked the rose and Christ's passion. Without wishing to suggest any direct influence (Lydgate had studied at European universities), we nevertheless find closely parallel associations in Storm in *Aquis submersus.* In all four references to nightingales explicitly singing, a four-fold image cluster is to be found comprising *Gott* (or *Himmel* or *Himmelslichter*), *Mond* (or *Mondnacht* or *Mondschein*), *Herr* (or *Herrengarten* or *Erlöser*) and *Nachtigallen.* Since one of the central themes of *Aquis submersus* is the conflict between the sacred and the profane, between art and life or illusion and reality, this heavy preponderance of 'loaded' biblical imagery begins to make sense. First, the moon association betrays typically Stormian ambivalence. Moonlight has a range of associations for him but it is most frequently linked with lovers' meetings and with passion. At the same time, he is clearly aware of its traditional association with danger (just as he is over the

dangerous associations of noon). In this he is only following tradition. The twin associations thus neatly dovetail
into the Philomela motifs of seduction and death. Linked
with these themes is the motif of the Saviour, reflected in
Storm's word-play with *Herr, Herren, Hof, Herrengarten,
Hüter* and *Erlöser* – unmistakable biblical imagery pointing in several directions: first, that this night of passion
is for Johannes both sacred and profane, as we see in his
call for his protector; second, the guardian motif itself is
ambiguous for it is reflected both by Herr Gerhardus, his
legal guardian and patron and Christ. This theme is struck
by Johnannes' guilt-sparked reveries, wondering whether
he will have to answer for his actions in the after-life not
only to Herr Gerhardus but also to Christ. Duroche rightly
points out that contrary to appearances this seemingly
genuine and sincere belief expressed by Johannes in a
benevolent deity is treated with heavy irony in the second,
shorthand language Storm is using particularly in expressions such as: *Aber Gott gab mir seinen gnädigen Schutz*[1]
antinomy. Such irony matches neatly the beauty versus
death epitomized by the nightingale, - an antinomy central
to this novella, centred as it is on the themes of art, painting, transience and death.

---

[1] But God gave me his merciful protection

We find confirmations of this view in the fact that Storm immediately juxtaposes images of death with each of these four nightingale references. The beauty of the birds' singing is confronted with the baying of the hounds in each of the first two references, with the bony, threatening hand (*gleich der Hand des Todes* in the third, and with the hard voice of the 'killer' Pastor in the fourth). Storm therefore underpins the Philomela legend in a variety of ways.

Apart from one other pertinent nightingale reference in *Es waren zwei Königskinder,* what remains of Storm's nightingale imagery is now restricted to *Ein Fest auf Haderslevhuus.* Storm strikes the pleasure-pain chord again in the former, with echoes of the cruelty of desire.

In *Ein Fest auf Haderslevhuus* the middle section of the story is dominated by a string of nightingale references. The associations are patently and unequivocally those of Courtly Love – of sweet longing and passion – of the headiness of love and *Minne:*[1] *du heil'ger Gott, das wäre ein Plätzchen für die Minne hier*! As the story reaches its tragic *Wendepunkt* in the last meeting of the lovers – a scene stocked with Storm's more melodramatic, mediaeval stage-props like the roll of thunder (*Gott hat's gehört!*), flashes of lightning, the watchman blowing his horn (shades of

[1] courtly love

Gottfried and Walther!), a final parting kiss, then silence
– the image of the nightingale becomes superfluous, a
point recorded by Storm simply as: *Die Nachtigall hatte
ausgesungen.* The bird imagery from now on is contained
in that sinister bird shorthand in which he excels – and to
which he is so prone – ill omens such as falcons, magpies,
eagles, vultures, crows and that sinister songstress – the
blackbird here singing out of season. Storm had earlier
established specific bird-associations for his two main
characters: the vulture is Rolf Lembeck's coat-of-arms,
by which he is finally identified and betrayed; Dagmar
is early on identified with the dove, a point driven home
by the murderous and suspicious Frau Wulfhild, who is
suggesting to Dagmar's father that he should fell the poplar
by her bedroom window. Later, when Rolf is invited to
the 'wedding' and finds Dagmar dead, Storm drives home
the bird-of-prey identification: *...sein Auge wurde wie das
eines Raubvogels.*[1]

As he leaps dramatically to his death from the battlements, clutching Dagmar's lifeless body, he exclaims: *Süße,
Selige! Breit deine Flügel nun und nimm mich mit dir!*[2] Storm
must inexorably press home his bird imagery to the last.

[1] his eye turned into that of a bird of prey

[2] Sweetest, blessed one. Spread your wings and take me with you

In his use of the nightingale Storm breaks dramatically with German literary tradition and picks up the alien literary and classical conventions of this bird as a bitter-sweet songstress. He is clearly familiar with the Philomela legend and exploits several of its themes, particularly those of seduction and death. Minor motifs, such as the nightingale singing itself to death, are also woven into his symbol fabric. Concurrently Storm employs the nightingale in its 'straight' mediaeval role as an emblem of love and passion, with scarcely a trace of melancholy. There is thus considerable ingenuity and range in his application of this most popular poet's image.

Storm is therefore not simply following a well-established literary tradition, with its roots in Classical Greece and Rome, in the *vogellin* of *Minnesang*[1] and the love-emblem of the Romantics. He uses the convention but also ranges much further afield. One senses that he was never really at ease in handling the bird, largely, one suspects, because he knew his readers' reaction to it would be a trained one and because the bird's conventional associations did not always suit his purposes. On the one occasion when he really works within the melancholy mediaeval convention (*Ein Fest auf Haderslevhuus*) the effect of his nightingale imagery is one of utter banality. It is only when

---

[1] the little bird of courtly love

he enters the second arena (the ominous birds) that his expert knowledge of birds and birdlore comes into its own and he is able to fashion his own symbols and symbolic motifs to high artistic ends.

We enter the second grouping of Storm's birds (the birds of ill omen) with some trepidation for we meet a highly sophisticated literary technique casting doubt on all optimism for most of the scenes met have to do with doom and gloom, with hostile communities, with betrayal and murders, with suicides, burglaries and rapes – the whole vast panoply of human criminality that likely passed before Storm in court in his capacity as a judge. As Storm aged his writing tended more and more towards the tragic workings of fate and in doing so gained immeasurably in tragic force and validity. This fine-tuning of his story-telling was to produce tales which projected him to world class status as a writer, notably with *Aquis submersus*, "Grieshuus: The Chronicle of a Family" and *The Dykemaster.*

Worthy of note is the fact that other writers of international standing have also paid service to this theme, notably, Daphne du Maurier, Salman Rushdie, Christopher Ondaatje, Edgar Allan Poe, Julian Barnes and Richard Burton seen in their Collected work: 'Birds Of Prey - Seven Sardonic Stories' (2010), so Storm finds himself in the company of Nobel Prize Winners. This underscores the need for Storm scholarship to finally come to terms with Storm's expert manipulation of wildlife.

The second, and larger, group of birds Storm exploits for literary purposes comprises the birds of ill omen, that is, all those birds which in mythology, literary convention and the folklore of birds are pre-eminently associated with the darker forces, - with the devil, with corruption and disease, with evil and with death. We have seen above Storm's habit of employing owls as hieroglyphic pointers to the macabre. One bird holds a position even above the owl and is pre-eminent in this group. That is the raven. In mythology and literature the raven has the right to be considered king of birds. Although Storm uses other birds of ill omen than the raven perhaps to greater effect, he is nevertheless highly conscious of the raven's demonic pedigree and generally conforms to the conventions surrounding this bird.

Reference to the demonic role of the raven as an underworld emissary of Wodan, God of Death, is particularly extensive in Germanic mythology and folklore. Its list of associations includes those of witch's familiar, *Hexenmeister*,[1] and magician. It is noted as a companion, emissary, apostle and steed of Satan, as a bird of the gallows (the site for the gallows was frequently called the

[1] sorcerer

Rabenstein[1]), of battles (both as an omen of the outcome and as a carrion eater) and, by its croaking on a house, as a bird of impending death. It had remarkable powers, according to early bestiaries and 'Natural Histories', for medicinal purposes, frequently in association with the corpses of murderers. Roman augurs generally observed the bird on the left hand and it was therefore ominous of evil.

Whilst the raven's reputation as a bird of doom and deluge and particular nastiness has survived virtually *in toto*, there is a second strand of tradition which renders its reputation a decidedly ambivalent one, a fact which Armstrong attributes to characteristic primitive modes of thought. He points to the whims and vagaries of supernatural power, which was thought to express itself either in benevolence or malevolence. As a consequence, a supernatural bird could presage good or evil. The twin strands of raven tradition may be seen as heathen and Christian ones, although Armstrong thinks it more likely that they arose out of man's need both to dread and cherish those objects which he assumed were invested with supernatural powers.

Storm extends the metaphor to its limits – not without a welcome admixture of wry humour. Gaspard, the private

[1] the raven stone

secretary, known as "Gaspard der Raabe"often assumes the role of jester in order to convey veiled warnings to Frau Wulfhild, his employer. This aspect of his character – his wisdom – is amplified by Storm, drawing heavily on the mythological convention of the raven as a bird of wisdom.

Storm is fond of attributing birds' behavioural characteristics to human beings. We have seen mention of the more obvious points about Gaspard – like his pointed nose *(Schnabelnase)* and the use of *aufpicken* in his search for clues, *spreizen*[1] of his fingers and *krächzen*[2] apropos of one of his observations *(18)*. His movements are also distinctly bird-like and he is credited with extraordinary powers of sight and hearing. Storm also makes a play on the word *Beute*[3] with its distinct overtones of the predatory bird. Although Gaspard attempts to avert the final tragedy and prevent Rolf Lembeck from going to his death, he had already played and cherishes those objects, which he assumed were invested with supernatural powers. On the one hand we have the bird as emissary of the God of Death, and on the other, as the embodiment of beneficence and the succourer of saints.

Something of this ambivalence of the raven's role in mythology carries over into Storm's work. Chronologically

---

[1] spread

[2] a croak

[3] spoils

speaking, one would have to start with the raven Krahirius in the *Märchen: Hinzelmeier.* In this tale the bird reflects much of the ambivalence it has for Storm. In one sense it is a bizarre figure of fun, a bespectacled caricature of the convention, in another it becomes an allegorical image of Death itself, in conflict with the forces of eternal life (in this case, youth). It is no wonder the 'Rosenjungfrau' chases away Krahirius from Hinzelmeier's dead body at the end of the tale. Similarly, in *Der Spiegel des Cyprianus,* as the murderous Colonel Hager clatters away across the drawbridge, leaving the Countess dying in her own blood, we find the comment:

> …dann…flogen die Raben krächzend
> in die Luft[1]

If one disregards *Hinzelmeier* and *Der Spiegel des Cyprianus,* however, as out of place in the canon of true Storm novellas, with the exception of the raven imagery employed for purposes of personification in *Ein Fest auf Haderslevhuus* (*Gaspard der Rabe*) one finds an exclusive use of sinister images in the remaining references to this bird. These allusions frequently double as death omens, death threats, macabre pointers and sinister concomitants of violent death. The sombre tale *Auf dem Staatshof,* is

---

[1] Then the ravens flew screeching into the air

neatly framed by an unusual copse of elms and silver poplars which are inhabited by ravens. Reference to these birds and their croaking occurs once at the beginning and once at the end (616), immediately prior to Anne Lene's fatal accident.

We find an unusual variant of this convention in *Schweigen*. Rudolf von Schlitz, the young forester consumed by the fear of developing insanity and seized by a growing compulsion to do away with himself, observes in the forest an old raven devouring the remains of a hare. The bird has no fear of him and appears to be safe from his gun. The ecological balance is disturbed, however, when Rudolf overhears an uncomplimentary conversation, muses on the theme of the runic inscription *Bis hierher, niemals wieder*! – and shoots the raven …*wie in gewaltsamer Befreiung.*[1] He shoots the bird not for practical, conservational reasons but for symbolical ones. As a *Totenvogel* (death) it is a reminder of the narrow dividing line between life and death, for the whole of this scene is saturated with frontier imagery – from the granite block with its runic inscription to the half-hare the raven is devouring, the midday break and the general juxtaposition of Life-versus-Death images: young hare versus old raven,

[1] as if in enormous relief

granite block versus living people, young birches versus dead old oak-tree and *schöne Lebensfülle* versus *Todesangst*.[1]

Killing the raven is an act, which has multiple symbolic implications. The bird not only symbolizes those dark forces which Rudolf thinks are taking possession of his mind, it is also an ill omen – as far as Rudolf is concerned – of the worst possible kind, an integral part of that web of sinister correspondences which has its genesis in the motif of the black flies, the rabid dog, the black type, the death's-head doodlings, the references to owls, a nightjar, a falcon and the bullet intended for himself. Killing the raven is a useless and unnatural act on the part of the forester, both a disturbance of the natural order of things and an outward manifestation of an inner mental disorder, pointing in one direction only – and that is death.

Zur Chronik von Grieshuus is a story of unrestrained and bloody violence, set at the close of the Thirty Years' War. The bird imagery in this novella is almost exclusively restricted to ill omens – to falcons, blackbirds, harriers, a tawny owl, crows and magpies.

In *Ein Bekenntnis* Dr. Franz Jebe leaves his house after administering a fatal dose to his incurable wife, to walk in the moonlit garden. The scene is permeated with death imagery. Jebe continues his account. His pet jackdaw is

---

[1] beautiful fullness of life versus deadly death

depicted in that unmistakable shorthand in which Storm excels, pointing to – or rather underscoring – death.

As a concomitant of violent death we find a brief but pertinent allusion to the raven in *Es waren zwei Königskinder,* in the final scene where Adolf and Franz stumble on the body of their student friend Marx in the forest and are startled from their sombre reveries into leaving the scene to make the arrangements for the funeral.

The role of the raven imagery in *Ein Fest auf Haderslevhuus,* however, is decidedly more complex than elsewhere in Storm's work, largely, one senses, because he has married to mythological allusion techniques of personification. In this novella is to be found Storm's most consistent use of bird imagery in the delineation of a character: called "Gaspard the raven" by the servants – not without a welcome admixture of wry humour, Gaspard, the private secretary, often assumes the role of jester in order to convey veiled warnings to Frau Wulfhild, his employer. This aspect of his character – his wisdom – is amplified by Storm, drawing heavily on the mythological convention of the raven as a bird of wisdom.

Storm is fond of attributing birds' behavioural characteristics to human beings. We have seen mention of the more obvious points about Gaspard – like his pointed

Schnabelnase[1] and the use of *aufpicken*[2] in his search for clues, *spreizen*[3] of his fingers and *krächzen*[4] a propos of one of his observations. His movements are also distinctly bird-like and he is credited with extraordinary powers of sight and hearing. Storm also makes a play on the word *Beute*[5] with its distinct overtones of the predatory bird. Although Gaspard attempts to avert the final tragedy and prevent Rolf Lembeck from going to his death, he had already played an instrumental role in bringing the tragedy about, for it was thanks to his detective work, that the girl was identified, and disclosure brought on her fatal illness. Gaspard therefore personifies many traditional raven attributes both mythologically and ornithologically speaking, with a very heavy emphasis on the sinister and the macabre.

In his use of the raven for sinister and premonitory purposes Storm reveals his complete familiarity with the convention. He is very much in the mainstream of a tradition which has its origins in Classical literature and has been widely exploited in western literature; one thinks of Shakespeare's facility in employing the ambivalence of

[1] beaklike nose

[2] pick up

[3] spread

[4] croak

[5] prey

the traditions, the raven motif in Sir Walter Scott's "The Bride of Lammermoor" and Edgar Allan Poe's poem "The Raven".

The function of the crow is closely parallel to that of the raven in Storm's work. The crow has been – and still is – frequently confused with the raven and is a bird of similar, if not identical habits and characteristics; it is not surprising that there has been some considerable confusion in the popular mind and perhaps as a result, the two birds share similar sinister associations. The crow is almost unequivocally considered by the superstitious to be a *Totenvogel* or 'bird of death'. Its cawing is generally interpreted as ominous, especially if a single bird calls from the roof of a house in which there is a sick person.

Of Storm's ten references to this bird, nine are specifically ominous and have explicit death associations. Typical of his technique is the fact that he mentions crows on six occasions in close association with either oak-trees or bare trees or bare battlements or a rotting well-plank, thereby fortifying their sinister implications. His reference to crows picking out the eyes of an executed infanticide in *Die Armsünderglocke* is based on long-standing folk tradition. The sole reference to crows which superficially has no immediate sinister connotations but which functions in an ominous way in the wider bird symbolism of *Der Schimmelreiter* occurs in the *Eisboseln* scene, in a few lines of remarkable plasticity – altogether a thumb-nail sketch brilliantly caught in the mind's eye.

Running with the raven and the crow in a very close second place in the sinister pecking order of mythology and folklore, comes the owl, as Storm clearly well knew. We find yet another of those occasional, explicit allusions to birdlore, as the story of *Der Spiegel des Cyprianus* reaches its tragic *Wendepunkt*. Immediately prior to the sudden mysterious death of Junker Wolf before the mirror, mention is made of a curious incident involving a flock of small birds and an owl, in which Junker Wolf describes it specifically as a Totenvogel. The allusion is typical of Storm's technique for it blends natural history neatly with Classical and Germanic mythology, whilst serving at the same time as audience preparation for the death of Junker Wolf, which immediately follows. It is typical of Storm's *Vordeutungstechnik*.[1] It is also an instance of Storm's accurate observations of the tawny owl, a predator which is frequently sought out while roosting by day by noisy parties of small birds, which mob it in an attempt to drive it away.

Mythologically speaking, the owl has been the dread of the superstitious since very early times. Its traditional association with death was noted – and used – by Virgil,

[1] technique of anticipation

Pliny, Chaucer, and Shakespeare. Goethe was clearly aware of its traditional role, for the owl is almost a minor motif on its own in the *Walpurgisnacht* scene in *Faust I*. In Roman and Germanic mythology its ominous associations were unequivocal as an image of death. Only the Athenians were out of step with these traditions in venerating the bird as an emblem of wisdom. The owl is one of Storm's favourite birds of ill omen, ranking second only to the raven in birdlore. Typically, he employs the owl ambivalently, both in a sinister way, preparing the reader for general *Unheil*[1] or more specifically for the death of a character, and also as a humorous personification. In *Schweigen* Storm quotes an explicit piece of birdlore, Classical in its origins but with a distinct Schleswig-Holstein flavour.

An owl sitting on a roof portending the death of someone in the house is an ancient superstition, which reaches down into modern times. In this context the marriage is clearly doomed. Storm is quite capable of quoting direct from oral tradition in matters of superstition – he does so frequently in *Der Schimmelreiter*, in particular, but quotations such as the one above, coming direct from birdlore appear infrequently in his work.

---

[1] a misfortune

Storm's use of the owl is consistent with his manipulation of the other birds of prey for sinister purposes.
We have already briefly traced above the owl's role as
Leichenhuhn and *Totenvogel* in mythology and superstition. His use of this bird reveals a broad familiarity with
many owl traditions. The bird appears as a premonitory
Totenvogel, its cry is ominous; it is used in a personified or
associative way with an evil character – *Herr* Bulemann in
Bulemanns Haus and Madame Jansen in *Im Nachbarhause*
links, and also for comic-grotesque effect with *Tante*
Karoline in *Beim Vetter Christian.* It sits on a house roof
and hoots – and the occupant goes mad in *Schweigen;* it
is associated with stormy weather and with *der nächtliche*
Graus[1] in *Waldwinkel;* its high position *in dem Haushalt der*
Natur is noted in *Beim Veter Christian.* Storm alludes to
this bird some twenty times yet somehow fails to exploit
the bird's full demonic potential. Shakespeare had demonstrated how effective the bird could be, drawing much
more extensively on the wealth of legendary birdlore
surrounding it:

"Hark! – Peace! It was the owl that shriek'd,
The fatal bellman which gives the stern'st good night."

The comment is made while the murder is being committed. In *Henry VI* Shakespeare has the King say: "The owl

[1] the nightly terror

shrieked at thy birth, an evil sign". But there are many other allusions to owl traditions, too – to the owl as a baker's daughter and a bird of wisdom: there are man's allusions to the owl's "five wits". Then there is reference to it as "the bird of night," breeding in dark places beyond the reach of the sun.

It is almost as if Storm shies away from the stock images – the familiar birds of ill omen, perhaps because he feels confined by the traditions, perhaps because he knows his readers' reaction to them will be a trained one. The answer might even be a much simpler, mechanical one: it is difficult to move this bird around in your narrative, since man's experience of it is largely confined to it's sitting still and hooting. So what conclusions may be drawn with regard to Storm's bird landscape? First of all, his range is both extensive and duplicitous for he touches on almost every aspect of birdlore, alert to all the sounds they make, to the colours they display and the variety of behaviours they exhibit. They perch and fly effortlessly through his scenery, an integral part of the majority of his later land-scapes. Personification is widely used, covering central aspects of character and behaviour. His manipulation of their duplicitous roles is superb for no other Poetic Realist can match him in this technique. Those birds primarily associated with death, destruction and deadly dénouement in his shorter novellas clearly play a key role and fit the tale's landscape with subtle yet sometimes fleeting effect. We can observe how the landscape within the landscape – death and destruction deftly wrapped in the seemingly innocent scene and the view within the view – appear through *our* binocular lenses.

Storm's close friendship with the Brehm father/son biologist combination together with their guided tour for him of Hagenbeck's Wildlife Menagerie in Hamburg reinforced and extended his knowledge of worldwide mammology. As for his birds, the only scholarly analysis and detailed study of Storm's literary use of birds is to be found in my 1978 work: 'Theodor Storm—Studies in Ambivalence', on which I have leaned heavily for the purpose of this updating of my theory. In the years that have elapsed since then, my original analysis has been confirmed and broadened to bring Storm under the new rubric of reading Storm's landscapes in a fresh light. For it is out of this highly unusual and richly fruitful confrontation that much of the latent strength of Storm's more interesting novellas springs, notably, in 'The Swallows of St. George', *Waldwinkel, Aquis submersus, Renate* and *Der Schimmelreiter* ('The Dykemaster').

Mention was made in Chapter I of Storm's very close affinity with his English contemporary Thomas Hardy. While Storm's fascination for and manipulation of birds is matched by Thomas Hardy's predilection for and extensive knowledge of insects, Hardy's limited deployment of birds helps to reinforce our reading of Storm's use of them, such is the great disparity in the way they handle them. For Hardy they represent a diversion, an excuse to expand on their migratory habits and the chance to elaborate on far-flung, exotic topographical regions as disparate as the Arctic and Africa, in other words as an opportunity for digression. Storm's birds are usually solitary, behaviourally accurate and in their duplicity, poetically highly significant.

CHAPTER V

Of Wolves and Death: Grieshuus

With the publication of *Zur Chronik von Grieshuus* in 1884, Storm produced a work which embodies virtually every aspect of his literary technique under discussion so far, notably his characteristic view of nature through his intuitively bifocal approach, peppering his landscape with duplicitous imagery affecting character, mood, plot and appearance. What is breathtakingly new is his introduction of an all-embracing and all-powerful nature motif covering his tale from first to last with its moral, ecological, historical and aesthetic implications. In choosing his wolf *leitmotif* he was tapping into a cultural icon

of enormous historical, mythological and literary proportions, all of which he was very clearly aware. The choice
was not fortuitous. The role of the wolf and wolves has
inexplicably received scant attention in Storm research.[1]
Examining Storm's presentation of this animal with a view
to determining what he wished to present in ecological and
mythological terms and how far he was reflecting the views
of his day – or even those of the 17th century is revealing
with regard to the motives for its inclusion. Traditionally
and culturally speaking, common attitudes to this animal
have been confrontational. In European cultures there has
been a predominantly negative view of the animal, having
biblical origins with demonic associations, fear and the
threat to livestock leading to the movement for extermination. Storm is exploiting these cultural responses to its
limits in *Grieshuus* albeit showing some empathy in the
cornering and killing of the last wolf. Ingrid Schuster
avoids the topic since much of her book, including the
Afterword, is throughout an animal rights manifesto. The
literary wolf appears in virtually all-European cultures
with particular prominence in Portugal. With Storm the
wolf connection is essentially one of a theme of protection

---

[1] Cf. D. Artiss: "Theodor Storms symbolische Tierwelt – dargestellt an
seinen Vorstellungen von Wolf, Hund und Pferd," Schriften der T.Storm
Gesellschaft, Band 45, 1996, pp. 7-22 (a discussion of Storm's symbolic
animal world with his perceptions of wolf, dog and horse).

and extermination – the removal of the threat to humans and the threat to the good governance of the estate.

The prevalent opposite attitude is reflected in American and Canadian literature where the wolf is admired for its strength, courage, hunting skills and its ecocentered capacity to live in harmony with man. If we accept Storm's prescriptive description for this work contained in the two words "deed" and "atonement" (*That und Buße*) the themes which surround them suggest a very broad canvas including war and the neo-historical, love and hate, family and fortune, the changing landscape and death and destruction all connected by the motif of wolf and wolves. The picture is invested impressionistically with all five senses of sound, touch, taste, sight and smell all emanating from a coherent centre, reflecting Storm's fascination with the arcane. With *Zur Chronik von Grieshuus* Storm managed to combine in 1884 all his skills as a dramatist, historian, folklorist, scientist and Poetic Realist in a work which was a precursor to *Der Schimmelreiter* four years later. Although it betrays elements of the operatic and of the romance novel as of Sir Walter Scott, it nevertheless shows his mastery in the development of the wolf motif, in his delineation of 'contemporary' history and in his development of the central character *Hinrich*. With *Zur Chronik von Grieshuus* we are confronted with a work unlike any other of Storm's for it is his closest approach to the short novel. It contains echoes of a wide range of genre characteristics, such as drama, tragedy, opera, the Gothic novel, the Sir Walter Scott romance, the grotesque, and, like Moll Flanders, the novel of character. It should be noted that this was not Storm's first literary excursion into wolf territory. Sitting as it was at the pinnacle of demonic superstition and folklore he was clearly captivated by all the possibilities it offered in dramatic terms for he was elsewhere to weave extensively around the image, to mirror wolf traits in human character. *Wulfhild* comes immediately to mind in *Ein Fest auf Haderslevhuus*. *Wulfhild*, from *Wulfkämpferin* – "female wolf fighter", for she betrays all those dark wolfish characteristics of cruelty, predatoriness, viciousness and wantonness, for woman's work at the spinning wheel was not good enough for her. She had used poison to finish off her first husband and she was not prepared to tolerate coarseness, nor infidelity in the second, but she was in fact more suited to the groom's father. As they cross the drawbridge to enter Dorning they are alerted to the howling of the wolves in the moat below. Rolf suggests having them put to death but Wulfhild will have nothing of Claus, whose heraldic emblem is a vulture, indicating the two together are arch predators. However, this mini wolf motif comes across as too contrived. Yet another instance of Storm's wolf predilections can be seen in *Draußen im Heidedorf*, where wolf imagery surrounds Margreth, the pretty Slovak girl with the pointed white teeth and black eyes, with more than a suggestion that Storm is playing with the notion of lycanthropy for the "white alp" of her Slovakian homeland had sucked out Hinrich Fehse's soul. His mother reports an animal peering through the shutters with sharp teeth and black eyes, suggesting, "it may not have been a real wolf". Hinrich also sees it, takes off and is found days later, drowned in a pond on the moor. Another instance occurs with the depiction of the murderous, aristocratic figure of Wulf in *Aquis submersus*, who is eventually killed by a dog. Of the twenty wolf references to be found in *Grieshuus*, which frame the tale from the beginning of Book One to the end of the Second Book, they tend to appear in regular 3-page sections, indicating regular and even distribution, in itself very consistent with the concept of a leitmotif. What is striking is the diversity inherent in Storm's exploitation of the many aspects of his wolf references. Fear of the wolf's threat to man is introduced at the very beginning. This brief reference alludes to a childhood occurrence of Hinrich's when in panic he had knocked on the gamekeeper's door, cap in hand and face flushed, producing the elderly man's response: *Was ist? Du hast den Wolf gesehen![1] und Komm mir so allein nicht wieder,*

---

[1] What's wrong? You saw the wolf!

Junker Hinrich![1] The stage is set and the threat apparent, fortified by Hinrich's admission that he had killed his dog in sudden anger for its unwillingness to join the wolf hunt. Storm pursues the joint themes of dogs, death and wolves relentlessly, bringing Book One to an end with the murder of Detlev. Development of the wolf theme has been essential to this point for much, if not everything, will hinge on bringing into focus the theme of wolf extermination at the very heart of the story. It serves to develop Hinrich's overcoming of his inherited character weakness of explosive anger through dedication and diligent pursuit of his goal, all albeit ending in tragedy. In the end he has successfully tamed the eagle/wolf predatory elements in his own character and through his dedication redeemed himself with *busse*. Storm uses several wolf confrontations throughout the novella to bring the different aspects of the animal into focus, namely the biological, the superstitious and the mythological thereby producing an image of the widest symbolic proportions. We are thinking here of *de griese Hund*[2] which had reputedly torn a day-worker's child to shreds or, with the neglect of the estate, wolves were seen coming into the kitchen, followed by the comment: *und über die Heide geht ein Spukwerk.*[3] Disruption of the

---

[1] Don't go out there by yourself again, Squre Hinrich!

[2] "the grey dog"

[3] and phantoms are crossing the heath

order of things comes with the account of a starving wolf stealing a recently killed deer. The howling of the wolves is directly associated with the perceived superstition of the "nugae". Storm even dips into the technical aspects of wolf extermination with Hinrich's accounting for his skills as Game Warden by shooting, ditching and poisoning wolves but also by lesser-known scientific methods. The training of wolf-hunting dogs is mentioned, as is the shooting of the last wolf. There is a sentimental touch in Hinrich's comment that they do not wish to let the surviving wolf pups starve to death, though they plan to bring them in and put them to death. With the Colonel's final comment over his son's dead body, Storm brings the motif to its conclusion: *Vor den Wölfen hat er dich bewahren können; der Wille Gottes it für ihn zu stark gewesen!*[1]

At the heart of this story are the conflicts between man and man, man and conscience and man and nature, with the notion of a 'Cain and Abel', guilt and atonement theme (Burns). Unlike the conflict between Hauke and the sea, which amounts to the central theme of "The Dykemaster", the motif of the wolves in this work, while threatening the lives and property of the *Grieshuus* estate, underscores symbolically the dark side of life and the theme of death, running throughout the tale. Many early interpretations

---

[1] he protected you from the wolves; the will of God was just too strong for him!

of the story focused on *Grieshuus* as a 'fate novella', only for this evaluation to be rejected by Storm just before he died. A much more recent one (Schuster) advanced the theory that nature in Storm is so critical that we should see Storm's animals as cyphers, critical pointers to his characters and their careers because, in this way awkward life topics such as biological, social and political issues could be concealed and poetically disguised. This, she argues, is Storm's secret narrative technique, forcing us to re-interpret 50% of Storm's fiction. Given that Storm's knowledge of the natural sciences is outstanding: in botany, dendrology, ichthyology, mammalogy and orni-thology, by compounding it with extensive cognizance of the role that flower, tree, wolf and bird plays in folklore, mythology and symbolism, negative and predatory and demonic images course through *Grieshuus* with great regularity, from black and white thorn bushes (demonic) to the parasitical wasps, both in the opening dramatic scene and to the elm and poplar trees (also demonic). Storm's outdoor scenes are richly invested in wildlife of great variety; they are nevertheless carefully coded and integrated, awaiting the sharp-eyed reader. The predators are almost invariably there. In the forest we meet as if by chance the polecat and the marten, both killers, then the falcon, vulture, eagle, crows and magpies, then blackbirds, ravens, jackdaws, all of which carry loaded, evil baggage in folklore and myth. If we see Storm's landscapes through his bifocals, we become aware of the second language with its own grammar and syntax, closely linked with the main text, complimenting events, character traits, all actions and moods. The linguistic overlap is subtle and sophisticated and one suspects it was either unconscious or instinctive on Storm's part, since timing was of the essence. Horses and dogs, the 'toys' of 17th century aristocracy, play an important role in this novella. Hinrich feels forced to kill his favorite dog because it baulks at joining the wolf hunt. Rolf's horse Fallada with mane and tail thunders though the final war scene riderless and as if possessed.

Philipp Theisohn's extensive discussion of all aspects of death (murder, suicide, accidental death, emotional and psychological death) with special regard to *"Zur Chronik von Grieshuus"* in his (Band 64 2015) paper for the Theodor-Storm-Society: "Über Leichen gehen" ("Walking over dead bodies"), in which he analyses not only all aspects of Storm's treatment of death (including murder, fratricide, assassination, suicide and psychological or emotional death) but also the heavy influence on Storm of Darwinian theory, asserting that death in Storm is always in association with animals, is not only very challenging but cannot be overlooked. A similar idea had been advanced earlier by Ingrid Schuster in her work 'Tiere als

Chiffre' (Animals as Cyphers), itself leaning heavily on my own 'Theodor Storm's Studies in Ambivalence'. Since death is present in most of its forms in *Grieshuus*, it would appear that Darwin's evolutionary theories surrounding the 'survival of the fittest' can be identified in Storm where predatory actions by man and animal overwhelmingly prevail. They appear to be part and parcel of the advancing pessimism of his declining years and the rise of a tone, which can only be described as sardonic, a development superbly analyzed by Nathalie Klepper in her paper 'Geschichtspessimismus und Gesellschaftskritik in den Chroniknovellen Theodor Storms (Berlin, 2005) Yet there are caveats to an exclusively one-sided interpretation. It becomes apparent that Storm was prepared to put a stop to any descent into nihilism by offering hope and the redemptive power of love as a counter to the depressing terrors of mortality. Storm scholarship has been remiss in ignoring the overwhelming significance of animals in Storm's work from *Immensee* on. What is new, Theisohn argues, is how Storm includes in his man-death-animal chain the transforming elements of superstition, second sight and blindness, the ghostly and intangible appearing under the term 'nugae'. Murder and 'animalization' belong together, and so he claims that '*Grieshuus*' is fundamentally a tale of animals—of falcons and eagles, of wolves and dogs, of domesticated and domesticatable animalistic power, reflecting "the problem of the sovereign". One could not agree more.

Storm's prose is highly evocative, creating a scene by simultaneously attacking many of the reader's senses of smell (in particular the scent of heather flowers on the moor) sight, (all the birds), sound, (the wolves howling), touch, (Hinrich and Bärbe) and taste – the numerous references to a variety of wines is testimony for the latter, so that the sensitive reader becomes 'lost' in the narrative, carried away to some sensual location limited only by his or her imagination. The twin themes of dogs and horses help to fix his free-ranging historical setting as cultural emblems of the aristocracy. They both occur from first to last in a role, which helps to regulate the narrative. The first dramatic scene opens with the recovery of the injured dog Tiras, the blow to Hans Christoph's head, and Hinrich's abuse of his horse in fetching the doctor, earning thereby Bärbe's ire. The twin themes of dog and horse are irrevocably intertwined. The dog motif is a central one, covering the themes of loyalty, obedience, protection, fearless and intimidating marauder control, and hunting, with their baying, location indicators. With a few brushstrokes Storm, the animal lover, neatly conveys both their utility and companionship with man. Fleeting mention is made of their names, Tiras, Hassan, Türk, Nero, their breed (bloodhounds and wolfhounds), their size and their coloration, underscoring Storm's attention to detail. At Hinrich's appointment as Game Warden, his two giant bloodhounds are ever present, earning a snobbish, derogatory sobriquet from the Colonel. The horse plays a variety of roles in the story both as the standard means of transport and communication and as a hunter in the extirpation of the wolves, as a teaching tool for the Colonel and his son and with a final flourish, Storm, ever the consummate ironist, describes Rolf's horse, Fallada, careering through the final military crime scene riderless and causing death, only to be captured and returned home, emaciated and completely demented, a fiery, apparition-like creature unfit for any further use, only to be finally dispatched by the Colonel with a single bullet to the head – a clear paradigm for the apple grey apparition horse at the heart of "The Dykemaster."

Storm made his intentions with this novella very clear when asked to explain them he replied with two words *That* and *Busse* (criminal act and atonement). *Grieshuus* is clearly not about the pessimistic theme of "the survival of the fittest" despite all the references to predator killers, including man himself, so in spite of Darwin's deterministic theories and studies in genetic inheritance, Storm pursues a different theme. Barbara Burn's searching analysis of the theme of guilt and atonement as opposed to that of 'crime and punishment' sets the stage for a more hopeful and empathetic resolution, in spite of the final destruction of the last two members of an illustrious family. On the issue of personal guilt and Storm's views on tragedy itself Burns writes: ..."four of the works (Storm) composed after 1881 differed from the others in admitting the possibility of a blemished individual. In *Hans und Heinz Kirch* (1882), "A Chapter in the Life of *Grieshuus*' (1884), 'A Confession' (1887) and 'The Dykemaster' (1888) the tragedy results not merely from irresistible forces with no moral implication but chiefly from character, from some aspect of personal guilt." This suggests Storm credits Hinrich's self-imposed and lifetime exile as a form of atonement for the act of killing his brother, bringing about his own redemption.

Much of Storm's great distaste for both war and a hierarchical, patriarchal society can be seen to be borne of his own life experiences. His experience living in Prussia left him allergic to the use of force by an all –powerful political state and left him with a very jaundiced view of Prussians. David Jackson focusses on Storm's bleak and deeply held Malthusian views in a passage of Storm's explicitly revealing his position. A shortened version in translation and central to our theme runs:

"What controls my mind above all – and that swallows up everything else – that is the disgust I feel in belonging to a society of creatures, which apart from the other functions ordained for them by nature, such as the search for food, propagation, etc., who with elementary stupidity pursue reciprocally each other's extermination. The world's survival rests in the fact that each one devours its opposite number, or rather, the stronger the weaker". (my translation)

Darwin's "survival of the fittest" is closely stated. The sentiments expressed above find expression in two works of Storm: *Eine Halligfahrt* and here in *Grieshuus*. In the former the elderly cousin has rejected society and retired to a purchased island offshore with his cat and pet sparrow to "cultivate his own garden". Though he is fond of entertaining family, he has cut himself off from all society, which he only holds in contempt. He is unafraid to die, lives in peaceful solitude with no room for politics, wars and a hypocritical society, completely uncomprehended by his female Cousin. In *Grieshuus* Storm's antipathy for war, destruction, devastation, starvation, rape and all sorts of violence is reflected in his accounts of the Thirty Years War and the Great Northern War – of many nations battling across Western Europe for power, from Sweden and Poland in the North to Germany, Austria, Holland and France in the South. His detailed scene of the Polish marauding soldiers, the intended rape of *Bärbe* depicts an accurate account of a world of marauding, thieving, death and destruction during those wars.

At odds with Burns' convincing position is one advanced by Ingrid Schuster, preferring the more cynical Darwinian assessment of Storm, holding that he concurred with the theory of "the survival of the fittest" and that that is what *Zur Chronik von Grieshuus* is all about. Her other challenge was to my book, when claiming to be the first to advance the ideas contained herein unacknowledged such as 'cypher' (chiffre) and 'ambivalence' (the original title being 'Studies in Ambivalence'). Much of that text dealt with animals and birds as cyphers – it must be patently clear. Her research into Storm's relationship with both nature and all animals and birds, both native and foreign and the history of Storm's intimate relationship with the father/son Brehms, and multiple mammal texts such as Brehm's popular *Tierleben*, however, is first class, serving to enhance my own interpretations. She rightly claims that Storm studies have overlooked the interaction of man and animals in his novellas and their significance as mirrors and catalysers. Advancing from my position to 'the animal as art figure', requiring a rereading of all the novellas, however, completely stretches her credibility. Insisting on a forced re-reading in the light of her own art theories is clearly unacceptable. Schuster's work merits considering, if only it contains some useful discussions of Storm vis-à-vis animals in specific novellas and in spite of its hidden agenda as an animal rights manifesto.

In conclusion Storm's portrayal of the decline in fortunes through the ages of a fictional aristocratic family seated at *Grieshuus* is relentlessly pursued down to the violent deaths of its last members. His social criticism of the aristocracy for their arrogance, sense of entitlement and ruthless abuse of power itself is consistent and virulent for he had described them to a friend as "poison in the veins of the nation". It comes therefore as no surprise that the story rebounds from one dramatic crisis to another with elements of unmitigated horror and dramatic irony. *Hinrich's* character flaw of sudden, violent and overcoming anger (*Jähzorn*) is something he brings under perfect control in exile over the years. He returns incognito as an old man, a chastened and charismatic figure, not to reclaim his rightful inheritance but to spend time with his grandson. The story is peppered with death imagery from first to last, masterfully concealed in those images drawn from nature, embodied in weather, flower, plant and tree, bird, dog, horse and wolf, in the erudite understanding of their unmitigated death role in folkore and mythology. This is Storm at his bifocal best. He perceived such natural phenomena as part and parcel of the 'poetic' elements of his writing. Ignorance of this special coded writing is not necessarily a reader's handicap, for the story operates so powerfully at the 'realist' level. In spite of the many interpretations, the fact that Storm considered the alternate title of the Junker (Squire) points to Storm's assessment:

that it is the true character study of one man with the fatal flaw of a very short fuse, who justifiably kills his brother only to send himself into a lifetime's exile yet eventually finds atonement.

It was Storm's avowed aim in all his tragic novellas that the reader should feel shattered (*erschüttert*) emotionally and temperamentally by reading them. Coloured by accurate historical culture and milieu, Storm the master storyteller has produced in the short form a masterpiece in European literature.

Conclusions

By reading Storm's landscapes we sought to bring to light
much that has not only been overlooked and at times
denigrated in Storm scholarship but to bring into full
focus powerful elements which are frequently central
to Storm's dramatic writing, particularly in the later
chronicle novellas. Until very recently the extraordinary
depth of Storm's animal kingdom, its all-pervading role in
his major novellas together with its reflection of Storm's
ethos has largely been dismissed. Two years ago an epoch-
making article appeared to rectify this situation. Philipp
Theisohn's 'Über Leichen gehen' ('Walking Over dead
Bodies') discussed the role of death in Storm's work with
special reference to *Zur Chronik von Grieshuus*, analyzing
the latter skillfully in the exclusive terms of an 'Animal

Story'. We have shown how the wolf motif dominates the tale, illuminating the central theme of the predator from first to last, symbolically embroidered by predatory birds, dogs, horses, wildlife, humans and weather. Ingrid Schuster had made similar claims in 2003, building on my own 1978 argument 'Studies in Ambivalence'. We have seen how Storm's landscapes as seen through the painter's eye are viewed consistently bifocally, in that sense the hybrid perceptions of the poet-realist. This fact alone, distinguishes Storm from all other Poetic Realists, moving him closer to Thomas Hardy, the Naturalists and the Symbolists. We have seen how Storm's range within his animal and avian kingdom is prodigious as is his manipulation of aspects facing the problem of time. The result is such that it would not only seem timely and appropriate in this Bicentenary Year of Storm's birth to recognize the timeless quality of Storm's work and deservedly elevate him to the pantheon of European literature as Master Poet and Dramatic Novelist.

List of Names mentioned in Text

Philipp Theisohn	Clifford Bernd
Ingrid Schuster	Heinrich Heine
Irmgard Roebling	Alexander Pache
Regina Fasold	Fritz Martini
Louise Forsell	Terence Rogers
Rachel Carnaby	Richard Brinkmann
Robert Pitrou	J.P. Stern
Georg Bollenbeck	Tilo Alt
Winfried Feund	Wolfgang Baumgart
Denis C. Jackson	Ernst Hebart
Thomas Kuchenbuch	Michael Irwin
Walter Reitz	Fritz Böttger

Johann von Goethe	Adalbert Stifter
Hermann Hesse	Conrad Meyer
Franz Stuckert	Wilhelm Raabe
Gertrud Storm	Jeremias Gotthelf
Walter Brecht	Annette
Oscar Wilde	von Drostehülshoff
Karl Friedrich Boll	Theodor Fontane
Ernst Jünger	Mao-Tse-Tung
Joseph von Eichendorff	Thomas Mann
Sir Walter Scott	Charles Darwin
Karl Müllenhoff	Thomas Hardy
Ludwig Bechstein	Karl E. Laage
The Brothers Grimm	Dieter Lohmeyer
Paul Heyse	David Jackson
Gottfried Keller	Nathalie Klepper

Lightning Source UK Ltd.
Milton Keynes UK
UKHW01f0613270718
326381UK00001B/14/P